The Trash Can of L.A.

A Reality Play

Jennifer Semple Siegel

The Trash Can of L.A.

ISBN-10: 0988624249
ISBN-13: 978-0-9886242-4-5

The Trash Can of L.A.

A Reality Play

Jennifer Semple Siegel

✳

Ban My Book Publishing

BanMyBook.com

Without art, the crudeness of reality
would make the world unbearable.

-George Bernard Shaw

DEDICATED TO

Edward T. Jones

who gave me the idea

for this play

COVER

Photographer: Roman Sinichkin

License: ShutterStock.com

Design: Jennifer Semple Siegel

Table of Contents

Table of Contents

(Continued)

About The Trash Can of L.A.

TILLY ZEACE, a homeless woman, has been approached by OSCAR FISHBEIN, a washed-up screenwriter, to participate in the first segment of TONY THORNTON'S new "reality-based" TV show.

STREET SHOCK, a Unicorn Studio Production, would feature each week a different segment of the underclass. For the first episode, TONY wishes to feature TILLY and other street people in a segment about the homeless; he and a VIDEOGRAPHER, armed with a hand-held camera, would follow TILLY around as she does what homeless people supposedly do.

TILLY is drawn to this project because she believes that the American public has a skewed view of street life, and she wishes to present another point of view. However, while TONY wants the final product to "feel real" to his audience, he also wants the segment to have a plot, so the studio has hired OSCAR to write up a script, one filled with stereotypes about street people and depicting TILLY as a shabby alcoholic and drug addict who has no choice about her circumstances. However, as OSCAR gets to know TILLY better, he slowly sheds these preconceived notions.

For a time, it seems as though TILLY will be able to present the "real Tilly as street person" to the American public, but a complication presents itself: the DIVINE MS. ALTA UNIVERSE, a

"New-Age" guru and the new owner of Unicorn Studios, adds her own agenda to the script; she insists on adding a scene in which TILLY converts to a new-age Christianity and abandons her "evil" life. Adding to this mix, TILLY eventually reveals that she is not exactly what she appears to be.

In the middle of this muddle, GINGER, a shallow young woman harboring her own ambitions and secret, shows up and complicates everyone's life even more, especially TONY'S.

TILLY soon discovers that reality-based TV has its own set of rules, so she must decide whether she wants to play by those rules or retain her unfettered way of life.

But then a dramatic change occurs, affecting each major character in some significant way; even so, this *STREET SHOCK* episode has limped along through production and is now ready for its debut.

What happens when *STREET SHOCK* is finally shown to a live audience? Will theatre goers/TV viewers get a genuine glimpse into the life of a homeless woman? What overall commentary does this play impart about American culture and entertainment?

Throughout the play, these questions are addressed, some implicitly and some answered in the "The Wrap."

For the overall societal implications for our culture, each reader/playgoer must arrive at his or her own conclusions.

The Players

(In Order of Appearance)

The Divine Ms. Alta Universe
(Owner, Unicorn Studios), 157

Male Actor (May also assume the role of Ted)
(Actor in episode of Street Shock*)*, 158

(Character descriptions can be found at the end of the play: "Playwright's Notes On Characters," starting on page 149)

Setting and Time

Setting

Take 1:
City street, outside Unicorn Studios.

Takes 2 - 10:
Stage, Unicorn Studios, Los Angeles, California

The Wrap:
In a theatre, before a live audience

Time

The Present

The Program

The Trash Can of L.A.

A Reality Play

Prequel

(While the AUDIENCE *is seated, still photographs from* STREET SHOCK, *a reality show produced by Unicorn Studios, are shown on the flat screens. Music, which should be bold and daring, perhaps something classical, such as Wagner's "Ride of the Valkyries," accompanies the stills. At rise, house lights go down. The music and street scenes fade out and go to black.)*

VOICE OVER

(Bold and authoritative.) The following program may contain some disturbing messages. Audience discretion advised.

(Silence.)

9

Take 1

(Stage lights remain down and curtain remains closed. On the flat screens on stage and throughout the studio, a grainy black and white scene appears, beginning with a close-up of TILLY, one of those facial shots which zeros in on her eyes, nose, and mouth—chopping off the top of her head and her chin—fades in. There is no dialogue, but "silent movie" music—piano or organ—accompanies this sequence; thus, all action is "mimed." The camera remains stationary for about 15 seconds. During this time, TILLY looks puzzled, as if asking, "What's going on?" The camera begins panning back until TILLY becomes part of a city street; she's sitting lotus style on the pavement, her back against a wall. Her hair is long and a bit messy, and, occasionally, strands blow across her face. Next to her is a tin cup, a satchel, and an overnight bag. Somewhere in the frame should be a trash can. She is looking up at and talking to someone off camera. Occasionally, people walk back and forth, blocking her from view.)

(OSCAR enters the picture, drops a coin into her tin cup, and stands over her, his hand on his chin. He says something to her, which obviously annoys her. She crosses her arms. They enter into an obviously animated conversation, complete with exaggerated body movements and language. She jumps up, and they start arguing about something. From time to time, OSCAR puts his hand on her shoulder or back, and she angrily pushes it away. Eventually, TILLY and OSCAR settle down into what appears to be a civilized

conversation. The camera zooms in and holds when the picture shows TILLY and OSCAR from the chest up. He hands her a business card: she studies it and slowly nods. OSCAR is obviously very pleased, and TILLY still seems a bit upset and confused. The two shake hands, and OSCAR exits. As TILLY continues staring at the card, the camera pans back until TILLY is but a long shot. Again, pedestrians walk back and forth, occasionally blocking her from view. While in view, she tosses the business card into the trash can but then pauses, retrieves the card, and puts it into her pants pocket and returns to her lotus position. The camera holds that frame for a few seconds and then slowly zooms in on TILLY's face, repeating the opening shot of her face, nose, and mouth. Holds for a few seconds, and then the picture and music fade out to black. Stage lights fade out.)

Take 2

(At rise, stage lights come up. TILLY wanders onto the stage by herself, as if she has been directed to come here. She is wearing her "dress-up" clothes, including a faux fur cape, her hair done up in a tight bun. Studies her surroundings carefully, noticing especially the old clothes hanging on the pegboard. Touches and examines them.)

TILLY

Good God! What's this world coming to, anyway? Who's minding the wardrobe department these days?

> *(Notices an old pair of galoshes on the floor next to the shopping bag. Picks up a boot.)*

Lovely footwear, Le Salon Goodwill, *n'est-ce pas?*

> *(Casually drops the boot onto the floor. With a flourish, throws the sweater over one shoulder.)*

The latest from Saks of Hollywood—or is that Fredericks?

> *(Tries on the hat. Poses.)*

Ooh, la, la! Ze latest, guaranteed to titillate *even* the most

---

discriminating man.

("Mimics" a runway model.)

Dahling!

(Stops in front of the table. Notices the poster taped to the table. Slowly, she reads aloud and rather dramatically:)

"Hold fast to dreams, for if dreams die, life is a broken winged bird that cannot fly. Langston Hughes." Hm-m-m.

(Removes the hat and sweater and returns them to the pegboard. Takes off her fur cape, drapes it on the back of one of the folding chairs, sits down, and crosses her legs. She pulls at the rubber bands on her wrists and then reaches into her satchel, and, ignoring the "No Smoking" signs, pulls out a pack of cigarettes, opens it, takes one out, and lights it. Takes a long, exaggerated drag and blows smoke toward the AUDIENCE.)

Well, so this is how television's done now. In my day—

(Notices the costume jewelry lumped together on the table and casually sifts through the mass of faux gold, silver, and gems. Perhaps for the sake of dramatic contrast, she could flash and twist her own tasteful ring.)

Who's supposed to *wear* this stuff, anyway?

(Pauses.)

Not *me*! Let me tell you that right now.

(Places her cigarette at the end of the table and sits back in her chair, folding her arms.)

So, now what?

(Pauses.)

Wonder who's minding the great Unicorn these days?

(Looks around.)

Not even a palm tree, eh?

(Picks up the cigarette and flicks the ashes onto the floor.)

What on earth am I doing here, anyway? You'd think I'd learn—

(Starts puffing away on the cigarette.)

(As she smokes, a phone rings. TILLY pulls a mobile phone from her pocket, looks at the screen, shuts it down, and puts it out of sight.)

Damn gadgets. Always yammering at you.

(As TILLY puts her phone away and continues puffing, TONY enters from SL. He strides to the other side [SR] of the table and, remaining on his feet, offers TILLY a firm handshake.)

TONY

How do. I'm Tony Thornton, director. You Tilly Zeace?

TILLY

Yeah, that's me. *(Reluctantly takes his hand but remains seated).*

TONY

(TONY notices the cigarette, but before he can say anything, TILLY tosses it into a coffee mug.)

(Nervously.) Uh, Oscar said you'd be by today.

TILLY

That little worm....

TONY

What?

TILLY

Oh, nothing, just talking to myself. *(Pauses and smiles broadly.)* Goes with the territory. Oh, by the way...*(Digs through one of her many pockets, pulls out a business card, and hands it to TONY.)* My website.

TONY

(Takes the card. Reads:) Zeace.com. How charming. So how do you access internet?

TILLY

Libraries are still free. *(Pauses.)*

Oh, yes, if you need some funky art, there's a link to my Artwork-y site. When I'm not being a bag lady, I'm a webmaster.

TONY

(Pulls at his collar.) I see. *(Checks his watch.)* Well, anyway, Oscar'll be here soon, but just to give you the skinny...You familiar with *Pawn Stars*, *Storage Wars*, or *Long Island Medium*?

TILLY

Nope.

TONY

(Laughs nervously.) Righto.

(Pauses.) You street people don't watch much TV, do you?

TILLY

Enough. Amazing what's available online. I prefer shows like *History Detectives* and *Antiques Roadshow*.

TONY

(Sniffs and sticks his nose into the air.) Bor-ING! All talk and no action.

TILLY

But very cerebral.

TONY

Whatever. But I gotta tell you, Tilly. The public can't get enough of reality shows. And *Street Shock's* gonna to change the way America watches TV and surfs the net.

TILLY

How so?

TONY

We're gonna put the viewer right on the street. The camera'll be his eyeballs, the cameraman his feet. The demo, uh, you know, demo-demo, uh, you know, those demo-whatchamacallits!

TILLY

Demographics.

TONY

Yeah! That's it. Demographics. Those things show our viewer's male and likes rough sports and lots of violence. Likes his sex down and dirty.

(Nervously.)

Not that we plan to do anything like that.

(Pauses. Then directs his remarks more to the AUDIENCE rather than to TILLY.)

It's really exciting, this reality stuff. You never know what's going to happen once you roll the camera. Like last week. We filmed a man jumping from seventh floor of the Capitol Records building. Splat! All over the sidewalk.

(Shakes his head regretfully.)

Couldn't air it, though. The big Kahuna says the show's gotta *(Mimics a female voice in a sarcastic tone)* "meet certain standards of good taste."

(Own voice again.) Happy endings and all that happy horseshit. Still, we can give 'em plenty of reality in between. *(Pauses.)*

And get this: the marketing department's workin' on a virtual reality and 3-D version of *Street Shock*. First, we hook 'em on prime time, and then we yank the show. Create mega blockbuster reality movies. Upload Youtube teasers. Develop video games. Build reality theme parks. Then...

(Becomes excited)

...GO IN FOR THE KILL! YES!

(Pauses. Calms down.)

The sky's the limit, Tilly, and you can be part of it.

(Pulls a contract from his pocket and unfolds it.)

All you hafta do is sign on the dotted line! Whaddya say?

TILLY

Depends. What exactly do you want from me?

TONY

Reality, sweetheart. Reality.

TILLY

Reality? You mean *my* life on the street?

TONY

That's it. Our first show'll be about you and all the street people in L.A. We'll call it "Trash Can Tilly," after you, the champion of the homeless. How's that? And you'll be our star. The camera'll follow you around, see, and you'll do what you usually do, you know, like go through garbage cans, beg, booze it up, snort coke, smoke crack, shoot up heroin....

TILLY

(Folds her arms and taps her foot.) Like a *real* homeless person.

TONY

That's it! That's it!

TILLY

(Gritting her teeth.) In your dreams...

TONY

What? *(Hears a noise and turns SL.)* Oh, here comes Oscar. *(Walks toward SL and returns with OSCAR. Pats him on the back.)* Oscar, my man!

OSCAR

(OSCAR pushes TONY away and immediately dominates the stage. He struts back and forth SC, totally ignoring TONY and TILLY, apparently looking for something.)

Where's my mug?

TONY

(Sticks his finger in his collar. Appears to be sweating. Inches over to the table SL and tries to hide the cup under some jewelry. Some of the jewelry falls to the floor.)

Looks like the janitor snagged it. There's foam cups—

OSCAR

FOAM? Did you say *FOAM?* Bite. Your. Tongue. Young. Man.

TILLY

(Smirking. Picks up cup and digs out some jewelry.) You looking for this?

(TONY closes his eyes and slaps his forehead.)

OSCAR

(Struts over to TILLY, takes the cup, and kneels before her. Takes her hand and kisses it.)

My dear lady, you're a lifesaver.

(Looks inside the cup and, without missing a beat, dumps the cigarette butt onto the floor. Gets up and pours himself a cup of coffee. Shakes a huge amount of sugar into the coffee and begins to drink without stirring.)

Ahhhhh-hhhh-hh-h....Just the way I like it: black, sweet, and *nasty.* Puts hair on my chest and everywhere else.

(Takes a long swallow and then looks at TILLY again.)

By the way, who the hell are you?

TILLY

(Folding her arms.) Who do you think? Kim Kardashian?

OSCAR

(Looks her up and down. Nods his head.) Close enough.

(TILLY jumps to her feet and starts toward OSCAR.)

TONY

(Jumps in front of TILLY and takes her by the shoulders.) Don't pay him no never-mind. *(Takes TILLY aside, SR, close to AUDIENCE, far away from OSCAR.)* He's a pig, 'specially around women. You'll get used to it. *(Consoles her.)*

OSCAR

(While TONY calms TILLY down, OSCAR pulls a script from the table and flips through it. Stops at a page in the middle. Without taking his eyes off the page, he drinks more coffee and freshens his cup. He finishes it off and sets the cup down. Then he begins to read in earnest. As he turns each page, his face gets redder, and he starts breathing hard. He winces and holds his chest, but only for a short time. He tosses the script onto the floor in disgust.)

Tripe! Pap! Why do I even bother writing such crap? *(Buries his face in his hands.)* I've sold out. My very own soul, down the shithole. *(Begins to shake.)*

TILLY

He didn't even recognize me!

TONY

(Pulls at his collar). Don't get bent. Half the time he forgets my name. Look. He's been scopin' out thousands of women, lookin' for, you know, a *real* homeless lady.

TILLY

(Shaking her head.) For reality based TV...

TONY

Yep.

TILLY

(Turns toward OSCAR who continues acting rather self absorbed. Reaches toward him, gesturing in an exaggerated manner.)

Look at him. A broken old man. An aging Lothario—

OSCAR

I HEARD THAT! *(Returns to his self-absorption.)*

TILLY

(Ignoring OSCAR.) Where did you dig him up, anyway?

TONY

Dig him up? Are ya kiddin'? Oscar's really talented, Tilly. See, in the heyday of TV, you couldn't touch 'im for less 'n 50,000 bucks a show. Stuff like *St. Elsewhere* and *Cheers*. And that was just for consulting. Lord knows what he got to write the stuff.

TILLY

(To the AUDIENCE:) No wonder America's so screwed up...

TONY

What?

TILLY

Oh, nothing. Just mumbling.

TONY

YES! By all means, mumble. *(Pauses.)* But don't forget: once we start rolling, speak clearly and look directly into the camera. Speaking of the devil, here comes *[name of VIDEOGRAPHER]*.

> *(The VIDEOGRAPHER enters SL laden with rolled up wires around his/her neck and a large, bulky camcorder set upon his/her shoulder. He aims the camera at TILLY.)*

TILLY

(Walks over to the VIDEOGRAPHER, studies the obviously outdated camcorder, and plucks at the wires.) Really?

TONY

(Laughs.) Never mind that equipment. It's just effect. Our playwright created us back in 1983, when such gadgets were state of the art. *(Pauses).* Our videographer is just being nostalgic. We have since evolved, and with each performance, we'll continue to evolve. *(Pauses).* We are forever in "present day."

> *(The VIDEOGRAPHER sighs, shakes his head, and pulls away from TILLY. He/she walks over to OSCAR and taps him on the shoulder.)*

OSCAR

(Startled. Once again, takes command of the stage. Stands up straight and rubs his chin.) Oh, it's you. Well, you'll just have to wait until the old hag gets here.

TILLY

(Raises her hand.) Excuse me?

OSCAR

(Struts over to TONY and TILLY, leaving the VIDEOGRAPHER holding all the equipment.) Now, what?

TILLY

(Salutes and clicks her heels, and then stands at attention in an exaggerated manner.) Hag, Incorporated, SIR! Reporting for duty. *(Remains at attention.)*

OSCAR

(Turns red. Seems off balance for a few seconds.) But you can't possibly be...

(Still at attention, TILLY nods, obviously enjoying herself.)

OSCAR

(Regains his composure.) At ease.

(TILLY relaxes.)

OSCAR

(Circles TILLY and looks her up and down, as if in a new light. Rubs his chin several times.) You sure?

TILLY

Mmm-mmm, let's see, now....

(Pats her hair, face, then her shoulders—brushes each arm and brushes briefly across her breasts—and pats her stomach. Runs her hands down her hips. Pauses. Then slaps each buttock.)

Yep!

OSCAR

(To AUDIENCE:) A wise ass.

(To TILLY.) You look different.

TILLY

I'm dressed up, if that's what you mean.

OSCAR

Hmm-mmm. Not exactly...

> *(Stands with his right hand on his hip and his left index finger on his lips. Pauses as if in deep thought. Then shifts his weight and crosses his arms.)*

But don't worry. We'll get it right. *(Reaches over and strokes TILLY's hair, perhaps a bit too inappropriately.)* The hair's all wrong.

> *(TILLY moves SR, away from OSCAR.)*

> *(OSCAR, obviously miffed at TILLY's rebuff, goes back to the table and pours himself another cup of coffee. Begins wandering around the stage, picking up props, putting them down again, slurping coffee, and mumbling. Occasionally winces and holds his chest. His actions should be a slight distraction, but not too obtrusive.)*

TONY

(Snaps his fingers to the VIDEOGRAPHER.) Let's get some test shots going.

(The TECHNICIAN enters SL.)

(The VIDEOGRAPHER unloads the outdated equipment and hands it to the TECHNICIAN, who exits SL with it. From his or her shirt pocket, the VIDEOGRAPHER pulls out a tiny camera and pushes some buttons. "Snow" or "blue" appears on the screens. The TECHNICIAN returns and takes his/her place at a computer and control panel, which controls the stationary cameras around stage and around the studio. In other words, the video equipment should be fairly up-to-date. Shots of the ongoing activity should begin appearing on the screens—the same scenes for each screen—but no sound, of course. These early shots should be random—occasional shots of the audience, the ceiling, half a face, etc. would be ideal— jerky, out of focus, at odd angles, out of kilter—as if the VIDEOGRAPHER were a musician in the process of tuning up his instrument. As the play progresses, the shots should become more focused, more specific, and more professional.)

TONY

(Motions to TILLY to come back SL, close to the AUDIENCE.) C'mere. *(When TILLY hesitates, he motions again.)* I promise I won't bite.

(TILLY obeys.)

TONY

Oh, you gotta do something about your posture. *(Directs TILLY to stand in a certain spot and then takes her chin and the back of her head in his hands.)* "Let the neck be free to let the head go forward and up, to let the back lengthen and widen." *(Demonstrates the Alexander Technique.)*

TILLY

(Slipping from TONY's grip.) What *are* you doing?

TONY

Just somethin' to help you move around on stage.

TILLY

I hardly think my role calls for any old theatre tricks....

TONY

(Seems distracted.) Mebbe so. *(Looks over TILLY as if seeing her for the first time and circles her, picking lint off her jacket, touching her shoulders, and looking square into her face. Then stops abruptly.)* Open your mouth.

TILLY

What am I, a horse?

TONY

(Sticks his finger in his collar.) I wanna check something out.

> *(TILLY folds her arms and sniffs loudly. But she obeys, opening her mouth wide.)*

> *(The VIDEOGRAPHER zooms in for a close-up of TILLY's*

mouth, which can be seen on the screens.)

TONY

(With horror.) Oh, m'god! You've got all your teeth!

TILLY

(With amusement.) Is that a problem?

TONY

(Slaps his forehead.) This'll never do! *(To the AUDIENCE:)* Oh, why me, why me???

OSCAR

(From across the room). Why, what?

TONY

(To OSCAR.) Oh, be quiet. I wasn't talkin' to you. I was speakin' ret, uh, uh, retortily....

TILLY

Rhetorically.

TONY

Yes, retort, retorti...oh, you know what I mean.

OSCAR

Well, excuse me. *(Starts fidgeting and mumbling again).*

TONY

Oh, woe is me....

TILLY

All this agony over teeth?

TONY

You don't understand. Homeless ladies aren't supposed to have all their teeth.

TILLY

Says who?

TONY

Says me 'n Oscar. Just ask any ten people. You'll see.

TILLY

Nonsense.

TONY

Just the same, if we don't fix the problem, we're in the toilet....

TILLY

Oh, don't be silly.

TONY

(Ignoring TILLY, he walks over to his director's chair and sits. Crosses his legs and folds his arms. Appears to be thinking. Then jumps up.) Say, no problem. We'll just yank 'em!

TILLY

(With horror.) Over my dead body!

TONY

Of course, you'd be well-compensated for your loss. Maybe even implants afterwards. *(To the AUDIENCE:)* God, think of it, Trash Can Tilly, the old toothless bag lady down on her luck. Sleeping in doorways, boozing it up, smoking crack cocaine. America will tune in as Tilly turns her life around, her toothless grin beamed coast to coast and over the internet....

OSCAR

(Pours another cup of coffee and walks toward TONY and TILLY. Puts his arm around TILLY.) There'll be no pulling of teeth.

TILLY

(Pulling away from OSCAR.) Damn right, there won't.

TONY

(Still addressing the AUDIENCE.) ...An Emmy for sure! Ratings through the roof! Reality Blogs! Adsense! Facebook! Twitter! Youtube trailers! e-books! Kindle! Marketing gimmicks!

Just think, Trash Can Tilly dolls, before and after her conversion...

OSCAR/TILLY

(Both stand up straight and look at each other in complete shock.)
CONVERSION???

TONY

(Turns to OSCAR and TILLY. Runs his finger around his collar.) Oh. I forgot to tell y'all. There's been a small change in the script...

TILLY

Script? What script?

TONY

Sweetheart, this is TV. You gotta have a script. You got exactly 10 seconds to grab the audience—blame the web for that—and you gotta grab 'em good. Else it's channel surf city. Why d'ya think we hired Oscar? His good looks?

TILLY

But...

OSCAR

(To TONY.) Tell me about this conversion shit. Whose idea was this, anyway? *(Acts as if he's about to leave.)* Well! I'm calling my agent....

TILLY

(Turns to OSCAR and pokes her finger into his chest.) Just one damn minute, here. You said nothing about a script. You said this would be a reality-based show. You said I could just be myself, and *(Pointing to the VIDEOGRAPHER)* S/HE would follow me around and record what I say and do....

OSCAR

That's right. The script's just a backup plan. You know, to fill in the gaps.

TONY

(Nodding.) And flesh out your character a bit. Perhaps create a composite bag lady....

OSCAR

About that conversion business...

TILLY

Just a minute, Mr. Fishhead...

OSCAR

Fishbein.

TILLY

Whatever.

(To TONY.) This is beginning to sound all very fishy to me.

TONY

(Shrugs.) It's done all the time.

> *(Frustrated, OSCAR walks over to the table and picks up the script from the floor. He flips through it and slams it shut. He rejoins the other two.)*

TILLY

Seems to me I remember a newspaper reporter years ago back getting into hot water for using a composite character in a feature story. The name Janet Cooke ring a bell?

TONY

Never heard of her. I'll Google her...

OSCAR

STOP ALREADY!

> *(Silence.)*

Good!

OSCAR

(To TONY.) Now that I have your attention. *(Shoves script into TONY's hand.)* Show me where that Goddamn conversion scene is so I can tear it out and rip it to shreds.

TONY

(Shakes his head.) No can do. This change comes straight from the top. Alta Universe herself.

OSCAR

(Puts his hands on his hips and glares at TONY. *Speaks slowly and deliberately.)* Just. Show. Me. Where. I. Can. Find. The. Goddam. Conversion. Scene.

TONY

Okay, Okay. *(Flips through the script.)* Ah, here we are. Page 45, middle. *(Points at the page and hands script back to* OSCAR.*)*

OSCAR

(Looks briefly on the page.) Good, God!

> *(Winces and holds his chest. Pulls out a handkerchief and wipes his forehead. Throws the script onto the floor.)*

TILLY

Who's Alta Universe?

TONY

Make that The DIVINE Ms. Alta Universe. She's our new owner. Belonged to that weirdo cult in Texas—

TILLY

Yeah, I remember them. They all set themselves on fire. What a mess. But—

OSCAR

Obviously, our Alta didn't hang around long enough to experience her baptism by fire.

TONY

Her WHAT?

OSCAR

(Sighs, rolls his eyes, and shakes his head.) Oh, just Google it!

TONY

(Shrugs.) Anyway, after the FBI got into the action and surrounded the joint, she dumped her old man and kids and took a flyer—straight to L.A. Somehow got a hold of the cult's money and bought into the studio.

OSCAR

How about that.

TONY

Then POOF! All hell breaks loose. *(Shrugs.)* The old man and kids all fried with the others. *(Laughs.)* A real Texas barbecue—

TILLY

(Disgusted.) You are *so* sick. I can't believe—

TONY

(Ignores TILLY. Wistfully.) Too bad *Street Shock* wasn't in production then. *(Pauses.)* Can you imagine the incredible footage?

TILLY

(Still disgusted.) Just plain voyeurism.

TONY

(Obviously confused.) What's that?

TILLY

(Ignoring TONY.) It's obscene, cashing in on human misery—

TONY

It's just showin' it like it is.

OSCAR

(Seems distracted.) Reality, just reality.

TONY

(Seems excited.) That's it exactly!

(Glares at TILLY.) Now where was I before I was so RUDELY interrupted?

TILLY

(Tosses her head back, folds her arms, and turns away from Tony.*)*
Harumph!

OSCAR

Our Ms. Alta's great escape into L.A. and her pilfering of cult funds.

TONY

YES! And it gets even better. Rumor has it, at one time, Alta's husband was a bigwig at Unicorn and left here with major bucks and stock options. When he bit the big one, he left Ms. Universe a bundle, so the old broad exercised her options and bought out the studio. *(Pauses.)*

A lotta big birds flew the coop. Others—

(Slices his index finger across his neck)

—got the old heave-ho. *(Pauses.)*

You just wait and see. You're gonna see lots of religious programming now. Dial-a-Prayer on steroids.

(Imitates a TV Evangelist. Very dramatic. Assumes the famous Richard Nixon stance. Loudly:)

Eleven buttons to salvation!

(Sings three times:)

1-900-I-m-Saved.
1-900-I-m-Saved.
1-900-I-m-Saved.

And a sexy URL...

(Chants three times:)

www.Keepeth.com.
www.Keepeth.com.
www.Keepeth.com.

(Returns to normal persona.)

New Agers rolling joints in the aisles, slick nut cases selling quartz crystals to the masses, wild-eyed cultists begging arms for hostages...

TILLY
(Walks to the folding chair where her cape is draped and begins to put it on.)
Forget it. No way am I going to convert in front of 100 million people.

OSCAR

(*Slides over to TILLY, removes her cape, and puts his arm around her shoulder.*) No, No, No, No, No. Relax. We'll get around it somehow. Look. I've been in this business a long time, and I know how to slide around crap like this. (*Pauses. Says thoughtfully.*) I could always sleep with old Alta. My wife won't mind if it's for a good cause.

TILLY

(*Pushes OSCAR away.*) You're insufferable.

OSCAR

(*Shrugs.*) Always good for a few perks, though.

TONY

(*To TILLY.*) Don't listen to him. He's all talk. Just ask Mrs. Oscar. Besides, the Divine Ms. Universe only sleeps with men in their early 20's. Says that old men suck the life forces from a woman.

TILLY

(*Snickering.*) Does she bathe in the blood of virgins?

TONY

I never heard that. Who'd do such a dumb thing?

OSCAR

Elizabeth Bathory. Said virginal blood kept her young and nubile. Also keeps the vampires away.

(TONY still looks obviously confused.)

TILLY

Just Google it.

TONY

(Shuddering.) Well, I hope I never meet up with that Lizzie chick.

OSCAR/TILLY

Not likely.

TILLY

About the teeth business...

TONY

(Looks at OSCAR who is shaking his head.) Not to worry. I guess that would be carrying realism a bit too far. Still, we could always blacken her teeth....

OSCAR

ENOUGH! Tilly is the chosen one, teeth and all. Let it go at that. *(Moves next to TILLY. Strokes her hair and begins to pull bobby pins from her bun.)*

(TILLY stands still as OSCAR continues pulling pins. Her hair falls to her shoulders.)

OSCAR

(Touches TILLY's face.) This is real.

TILLY

(Runs her fingers through her hair and studies OSCAR as if seeing him for the first time.) Yes, very real.

TONY

(Distracted.) Well, good. *(Pushes past OSCAR and motions to the VIDEOGRAPHER.)* Hey, you! I want to get some interview shots. *(Walks over to the two folding chairs and brings them down SC.)* Here we are. *(Motions for TILLY to sit.)*

(VIDEOGRAPHER starts focusing in on TILLY. Her image should be appearing on the screens.)

TILLY

(Looks away from OSCAR and turns red. Sits. Folds her hands and looks down into her lap.) Thanks.

OSCAR

(Watches TILLY as she sits down. Then goes to the coffeepot. The pot is empty or nearly empty.) DAMN!

(OSCAR exits SL, carrying his coffee mug. Stage lights go down and screens fade to black.)

Take 3

(Stage lights come up and screens come on. TONY and TILLY are still seated in their chairs. The VIDEOGRAPHER and TECHNICIAN are on stage as well.)

TONY

Now, don't be nervous. I'm just going to interview you, to see how ya come across on the tube.

TILLY

'Kay. *(Looks over her shoulder at where OSCAR has exited. Sighs.)*

TONY

None of these scenes'll appear in the show. Okey dokey. Ready?

(TILLY nods.)

TONY

Okay. One. Two. Three. ACTION!

(Points at the VIDEOGRAPHER who has long since started recording.)

(TONY straightens his tie and pulls at his collar. Shifts his weight around. Then assumes a phony persona, perhaps a Saturday Night Live *Weekend Update anchor imitation.)*

Anthony Thornton reporting for Unicorn Studios. I have here with me today Ms. Tilly Zeace, of, ha, ha, no fixed address, is that right?

TILLY

(Looks at TONY oddly.) Yes.

TONY

Could you tell our viewing audience why that is, Ms. Zeace?

TILLY

You may call me "Tilly," Tony. It's okay. To answer your question, I'm homeless. I live on the streets of L.A. I guess you could call me a bag lady because all I own can be found in this satchel *(holds it up)*, plus an overnight bag.

TONY

Truly an American tragedy!

TILLY

(Shrugs.) Depends how you look at it.

TONY

Well, uh, maybe you can give the viewing audience some background, a glimpse into the making of a bag lady.

TILLY

Actually, I had a very ordinary childhood—two parents, a sister, a dog named Rex. I grew up in a suburb near Philadelphia.

TONY

Then something went terribly wrong...

TILLY

Oh, no, not at all. I lived a charmed life. Good clothes, nice vacations, the best private schools. Great parents. Both are still alive. And I was not abused. *(Waves to the camera.)* Hi, Mom and Dad.

TONY

I see. What did you do after high school?

TILLY

Enrolled at USC. Film school.

TONY

You went to USC?

TILLY

I was there for a year...

TONY

AHA! A college dropout.

TILLY

Just for a while to clear my head. It was a volatile time in history, after all. Lots of cheap dope...

TONY

...which got you started on your lifelong drug and alcohol addiction. *(Stage whisper to TILLY.)* Just go along. It's all in Oscar's script.

> *(OSCAR enters SL with his coffee mug in one hand and GINGER hanging on his other arm. While TONY and TILLY talk, OSCAR motions GINGER to make coffee. Her chin in the air, she ignores him, posing with her hands on her hips. Then she pulls her mobile phone from her hip and starts texting.)*

TILLY

(Frowns. Ignoring TONY's order.) Addiction? Me? Are you kidding? Actually, I went back to school. Goddard College.

TONY

I've heard of that place. It's that hippie school in Massachusetts.

TILLY

Vermont.

TONY

(Annoyed.) Whatever.

OSCAR

(Puts his arm around GINGER and guides her SC.) My friend David Mamet graduated from Goddard...Must be a good school.

TILLY

(Turns around. Sees GINGER and OSCAR hanging all over each other. Is visibly upset. Crosses her arms and faces TONY.) DAMN RIGHT IT IS!

TONY

(To OSCAR:) How do you know this stuff?

OSCAR/TILLY

JUST GOOGLE IT!!!

TONY

(Assumes real persona. To TILLY:) Whoa! Didn't mean to upset you. Just trying to find an angle.

OSCAR

(Gently pushes GINGER away. To TONY:) Maybe you're trying too hard. Here, let me try.

(Gently pulls TONY from his chair.) Go see what Ginger needs.

(Sits down and faces TILLY.)

TONY

(Turns and smiles broadly.) Well, hel-lo, Ginger. Where did 'ole Oscar pick you up?

GINGER

(Haughtily.) I was told about a role for *Street Shock*.

TONY

Well, you've come to the right place. You want something to drink?

GINGER

(In a deep, sultry voice.) You have Perrier?

TONY

(Obviously excited.) I think that can be arranged.

(TONY leads GINGER SL. They exit.)

OSCAR

(Takes a sip of coffee and sets the mug down next to his chair.) Terrible stuff. *(Holds his chest.)* No wonder my heart feels like a jackhammer.

TILLY

(Concerned. Leans toward OSCAR.) You okay?

OSCAR

(Alarmed.) What are you, my mother?

TILLY

I'm sorry, I just...

OSCAR

No, No. It's okay. *(Takes TILLY's hand.)* I don't mean to be such a shit, but when you get to be my age, well, days are measured in teaspoons.... *(Pauses and stares at TILLY who seems a bit confused.)* But how would you understand? Look, let's start over.

TILLY

Okay.

OSCAR

And let's forget about that mumbo-jumbo childhood shit. Tony's such a dick, sometimes. Always looking for the angle, the easy answer. That's what *Sesame Street,* Facebook, Youtube, Twitter's done to his generation. Everything packaged in flashy 5, 10, 20, 30-second sound bites. No attention span.

(Studies TILLY.)

But he'll be okay, once he smooths out the rough edges and stops being so anal. Reminds me a little of myself when I was starting out in the business. More ambition than talent. 'Course, that comes or you don't last. But first you got to have that burning desire to be a somebody, and, in my day, you had to do some things you really didn't want to do. You didn't even think about it, you just gritted your teeth and closed your eyes. No such thing as sexual harassment.

(Pauses. Gets up and kneels before TILLY.)

You're lucky, Tilly. You get to be yourself, no matter what. I'll see to that.

(Winces and rubs his chest.)

TILLY

(Frightened.) Oscar!

OSCAR

(Relaxes.) It's okay. Just some funny beats. Happens all the time. *(Pats TILLY's hand.)* Don't worry. I'm from sturdy German stock. The Nazis couldn't kill my family, so why should a few fast heartbeats? *(Returns to his chair and folds his arms.)* Now, tell me about yourself.

TILLY

(Shrugs.) I don't know where to begin.

OSCAR

How about your life after Goddard?

TILLY

I went back to California to look for an old boyfriend. Stoney.

OSCAR

Stoney? *(Scratches his chin.)* Name sounds familiar. Maybe I know him.

TILLY

(Shakes her head and smiles.) I doubt it. He was into pharmaceuticals—you know *(waving the peace sign in front of her face)*, "Better living through chemistry"—not show biz. Besides, any guy with long hair and a taste for contraband was a Stoney.

(Pauses. Shifts around in her chair.) After I dumped Stoney, I couldn't get him out of my mind, and I thought maybe I could find him again, and, you know, start over. But he'd just vanished. POOF! Into thin air. Never did find him. Now I figure he's either dead or born again, which is the same thing as being dead.

(Pauses.) By the time I realized I wasn't going to find Stoney, I was broke and hungry. I had to find a job like fast. Believe it or not, I was quite a looker in those days....

OSCAR

(Leans close to TILLY.) Still are.

TILLY

(Shifts away from OSCAR.) But not in the same way. *(Pauses.)* I answered an ad in the *L.A. Free Press (assumes a dramatic pose)*: "Wanted: Sex Kittens for The Leopard Club." I applied and got the job on the spot.

OSCAR

How about that.

TILLY

Yeah. But I really blew it.

OSCAR

How so?

TILLY

Within a week, I got fired.

OSCAR

Fired?

TILLY

(Looks as if she's about to cry. Snaps the rubber bands on her wrist.) It was so dumb!

OSCAR

(Pats TILLY's hand.) What happened?

TILLY

(Definitely on the verge of crying.) It was late Saturday night, and I was dead tired from being on my feet for six straight hours. And you've got to understand the kind of costumes we had to wear. Skimpy leopard outfits. Fishnet stockings, a long tail.

(Brushes her shoulders.) No straps *(hands under her breasts)*, just cups holding us.

I'm serving pitchers to a table of Catholic priests. Can you imagine? I'm not paying attention—guess I'm daydreaming—and bend over instead of stooping. *(Stands up and mimes what happens when a "Sex Kitten" bends over.)* And my left you-know-what *(points to her breast)* spills out and ends up in a pitcher.

OSCAR

Ouch!

TILLY

There's more. One of the priests, an old man—at least 60—grabs my *(points to her chest)* and starts licking. I'm, like, in shock and just stand there taking it. When I finally come to my senses and push him away, he slaps me and says, "I paid for it." *(Starts to sob.)*

OSCAR

(Puts his arms around TILLY and comforts her.) Hey, hey. It's okay. That was a long time ago. There, there. *(Pauses, but continues comforting her.)* Besides, the old fart's probably fertilizer by now. Rotting away in his Roman collar.

TILLY

(Smiles and wipes her eyes. Frowns.) I just felt so dirty. Like trash.

OSCAR

It wasn't your fault.

TILLY

HA! *(Points to herself.)* Trash Can Tilly. *Spreads her arms wide, runs around the stage, and shouts.)* Hey, world! Meet the trash can of L.A.

OSCAR

(Spreads his arms out, pivots around, and looks all around the set and out into the AUDIENCE. Then he kicks the small wire trash container across the stage and pounds on the table. He stomps around the stage, points toward the AUDIENCE, and shouts:) YOU'RE THE REAL TRASH CAN! *(Pause.)* DO YOU HEAR ME? *(House lights come up. Points directly at members of the AUDIENCE.)* YES! I MEAN YOU! YOU! AND YOU! *(He freezes as if in tableau. Pause. House lights dim. He unfreezes and assumes a gentler tone. Shakes his head.)* Garbage in, garbage out.

TILLY

(Ignoring OSCAR.) Tossed out like yesterday's newspaper. Garbage. The worst part, my boss wouldn't listen. He accused me of hooking on the side. Can you imagine? I tried telling him I wasn't, as he put it, "fraternizing with the customers," but he shut me out. Looked right through me when he fired me. *(Pauses. With anger.)* I get mauled on the job; *I'm* the one who gets bounced—just like that.

OSCAR

He wouldn't get away with that now.

TILLY

I just wanted him to listen. So, okay, fire me. But, for God's sake, treat me like a human being and listen for a few minutes. *(Pauses.)* You know, *(hesitating)* I never worked again after that. Went right from the lounge to the street. *(Pauses.)* I get respect on the street.

OSCAR

Respect?

TILLY

Oh, I know what you're thinking. That people look right through us when they pass by us on the street, and that's true enough, but at least we know it's real when someone *does* acknowledge our existence.

OSCAR

Why do you think that is?

TILLY

(Pauses for a few seconds.) Because folks don't have to be nice. They know we've got nothing tangible to give back.

OSCAR

I'm not so sure about that. Right now, you're given me a whole lot to think about.

TILLY

(Surprised.) Really? How so?

OSCAR

(Shrugs.) You've shaken up this old dog's narrow view of the world. See, when I first saw you on the street, I couldn't figure out why you were so pissed off *at me*. I thought I was offering you a chance of a lifetime. I made certain assumptions...

(Obviously embarrassed.) I pegged you as a desperate, unhappy person who needed rescuing. That I was doing you a big favor by asking you come here. *(Pauses.)* But that's not the case at all, is it?

TILLY

(Shakes her head.) No. I choose to live my life the way it is. It's who I am, and I'm content with things the way they are. I don't really need this gig to fill any void in my life. There is no void. At one

time, well, maybe—

But that was a long time ago, another life—

OSCAR

If I died today, I'd go an enlightened man—

TILLY

Please don't talk that way! It's so morbid.

OSCAR

Oh, but it's true. Just don't tell Mrs. Fishbein. She couldn't stand any sudden enlightenment on my part. *(Laughs. Laughter slowly dies away. Silence. Shakes his head.)* Until now, I have felt so alone. Like I've been ignored on purpose just because I'm an old has-been, hack screen writer.

TILLY

The thing is, even when we're being ignored, we *are* being heard. *(Pauses and points at the AUDIENCE.)* Their silence speaks volumes.

OSCAR

(Thinks for a few seconds and nods.) Yes. It's becoming clear now.

TILLY

Now don't ever forget it.

OSCAR

I won't. And Tilly?

TILLY

Hmmm?

OSCAR

You *WILL* be heard loud and clear on *Street Shock.*

TILLY

(Pauses.) Maybe.

OSCAR

C'mon. *(Puts his hand on the back of her neck. She doesn't move away.)* Let's take a break.

(TILLY nods. She and OSCAR get up and exit SL. OSCAR returns alone and heads for the script he has tossed onto the floor. He picks it up, flips through it, and slowly tears out about five pages crumpling each page into a ball and dropping it to the floor. When he is finished, he winces, drops the script to the floor, and clutches his chest. He exits SL. Stage lights go down and screens shut off.)

Take 4

(Stage lights come up and screens turn on. The VIDEOGRAPHER and TECHNICIAN are already on stage. TONY and GINGER enter SL and proceed to down SC. Both are carrying half full containers of Perrier and are hanging all over each other. They are disheveled, giving the impression that they have been doing more than just drinking expensive fizzy water.)

TONY

Honey, we'll continue this conversation later. How about my place?

GINGER

(Testily.) What about that part?

TONY

(Pulls GINGER close, musses her hair, and kisses her forehead.) Don't worry. It's a done deal. *(Looks around the stage and scratches his head.)* Where the hell are they, anyway?

GINGER

(Ignores TONY's question.) I'm holdin' ya to it, bub.

(OSCAR and TILLY enter arm-in-arm SL, looking very smug.)

TONY

Huh? Oh, no problem. *(Notices OSCAR and TILLY, who are laughing and joking around.)* Oh, there they are. Look. I need a word with 'em. You just hang out 'til I need you. *(Kisses her lightly on the lips.)*

GINGER

(Sets the water bottle on the table and puts her hands on her hips.) I'll be waiting.

(GINGER moves far SR and begins doing warm up exercises, working her way up to full aerobics and running in place. Should exude excessive energy, but far on the sidelines.)

TONY

(To the AUDIENCE:) Whew! *(Hands shaking, he takes out his handkerchief, wipes his forehead and shakes his head.)* What a tough babe. Drives a hard bargain. Can't figure out why casting sent her over. Oh, well, I'll worry about her later.

(TILLY and OSCAR join TONY down SC.)

TONY

(Suspiciously.) Where've you two been, anyway?

(OSCAR and TILLY look at each other and laugh.)

TONY

A little hanky panky, eh?

OSCAR

Hardly. Got called in by our fearless leader. She wanted to check out Tilly.

TILLY

(To AUDIENCE:) I swear I know that Alta Universe woman from somewhere.

TONY

Well, does our star pass?

TILLY

(To AUDIENCE:) And she kept looking at me funny. As if she knew me, too—

OSCAR

(Shrugs.) With Alta, who knows? *(Pauses.)* But she told us something interesting about Ginger.

TONY

Is that a fact? *(Seems distracted. Motions the VIDEOGRAPHER to move around more. Now seems excited. To TILLY.)* Say, I think I've been approaching this whole thing wrong. See, I been doin' all the talking. I haven't gave you the chance to be the real you. Well, I'm gonna fix that. *(Takes TILLY's hand.)*

TILLY

(Pulls her hand away.) Aren't you at all curious about Ginger?

TONY

It can wait. Listen. I got a great idea. *(Shouts.)* Kill the lights!

(As the stage lights dim, a spotlight shines on TONY and TILLY.)

(OSCAR and GINGER cannot be seen.)

(TONY slides arm around TILLY's shoulder.)

(TILLY seems nervous.)

Now don't be afraid. It's just you and me, and I'm leavin' in a minute. Now close your eyes.

(TILLY obeys.)

That's it. Okay. Now relax. No, no. You're still too tense. *(Kneads her shoulders.)* Better now. Clear your head just like the gurus say. Okay. Lookin' good. Oh, shit, I forget what comes next.... *(Shouts.)* OSCAR! Help me out on this!

OSCAR

(Over a LOUDSPEAKER.) For God's sake, Anthony Thornton! Get with the program.

TONY

Please?

OSCAR

(With a deep sigh.) Okay. But I'm not doing it for you. And don't forget. You owe me one!

TONY

You got it! *(Hugs TILLY and exits.)*

OSCAR

Tilly? Can you hear me?

TILLY

Yes.

OSCAR

Good. Now Tony wants you to go back in time and visualize a defining moment in your life....

TILLY

Well, getting fired would be right up there....

OSCAR

I know, sweetheart, but let's try for something different.

TILLY

Well, okay. *(Pauses.)* I'm thinking.

OSCAR

Take your time.

TILLY

Much of my life—even my street life—has been dull as white bread. *(Pauses for a few seconds.)* Hmmm..., no that's too silly. *(Pauses some more.)* And that didn't really define my life. *(Pauses. Her demeanor changes, and she seems to "slump" in some sort of despair.)* Oh, that—

OSCAR

Good. Now, think about the scene for a few seconds and then start talking like it's happening right now.

TILLY

But—

OSCAR

Just a short dramatic monologue.

TILLY

(Alarmed, she puts her hand to her neck.) But it's really kinda personal.

OSCAR

Don't worry. This is off the record.

(To the VIDEOGRAPHER and TECHNICIAN:)

[ACTORS' First Names], please turn off the equipment and leave the area.

(The screens go black, and the VIDEOGRAPHER and TECHNICIAN exit SL.)

Better?

TILLY

Yes, thanks.

OSCAR

Okay, now give it a try.

TILLY

Well, let's see...Okay. *(Pauses. The spotlight intensifies and covers a smaller area of the stage.)*

You promise not to get mad at me?

OSCAR

Any reason why I should?

TILLY

(Hesitant.) It's just, uh...I haven't exactly been up front about some things—

OSCAR

You and about seven billion other people. Don't worry, Tilly. There's nothing you could say to tick me off.

TILLY

Well, then. You asked for it. *(Pauses.)*

You alone?

(Some crackling noises and feedback on the speaker—as if someone were covering a microphone and talking in the background.)

OSCAR

It'll be just Tony and me. I've cleared the area of everyone else. Okay?

TILLY

(Pauses.) Yeah. And thanks. Now I'm ready.

(Spotlight goes down.)

Take 5

(Spotlight comes up and focuses down SC on TILLY. She is standing.)

TILLY

(Begins speaking without much emotion. To AUDIENCE:) I'm alone in Schwab's Pharmacy, eating my melt and fries. I've just turned in my Sex Kitten costume at the Leopard Club, and I'm feeling a little depressed right now. I've got no one to talk to, but I feel a little better just being here.

(Pauses and looks around.) Take away the star-struck mystique, and Schwab's just another joint in tinsel town, where ordinary people like me hang out. *(Pauses.)* I come here because I like their food—Patty Melts with extra cheese and onions.

(Pauses. Still soft-spoken, but her voice seems to quiver a little.) I'm minding my own business, when a man stops by my table.

(TED enters the spotlight. He and TILLY remain standing.)

TED

Hello, miss. I'm Ted Andrews. *(Holds out his hand, but TILLY refuses to shake it.)* I'm sorry to disturb your dinner, but I just couldn't help but notice how striking you are.

(Offers her a business card.)

TILLY

(Refuses the card. Becomes very cocky. To AUDIENCE:) I'm thinking, "Yeah, sure, I've heard that line at least a thousand times, and, like, I'm going to fall for it now."

(To TED:) Get lost! *(Turns away from him.)*

TED

(Jumps around to face TILLY. Pushes the card into her hand.) But you don't understand. I'm a producer.

TILLY

(Reluctantly takes the card and looks at it. Reads:) "Theodore Andrews, Producer. *The Gathering Storm.* Unicorn Studios."

(To AUDIENCE:) Can you imagine? Unicorn Studios? Sheesh! *(Laughs as if she's enjoying the coincidence.) The Gathering Storm.* A TV soap opera. But I know all about the scam. Print up a thousand bogus cards, hand 'em to a thousand naïve girls, and if you're lucky, twenty'll answer. Twenty ambitious girls willing to do anything for that big break in Hollywood.

(Drops the card onto the floor.)

(To TED:) As I said before, GET LOST!

TED

I like you. I like sassy women.

TILLY

(Pauses. No longer cocky. Seems more vulnerable.)

(To AUDIENCE:) The thing is, he's not oily and slimy.

(Picks up the card from the floor and looks at it again.)

There *is* something appealing about him, but I also know that Hollywood wolves come in many guises.

(To TED:) Cut to the chase, and state your business.

TED

I'd like you to audition for a role on *The Gathering Storm*. You ever act?

TILLY

Just at Goddard College. I played Ophelia.

TED

Excellent!

TILLY

Why me?

TED

(Shrugs.) You have the right look.

TILLY

Me and about 500 other women.

(To AUDIENCE:) I tell him that I know all about perverts who prey on desperate young girls looking for roles and I wasn't really thinking about an acting career anyway.

(To TED:) So you see, you're wasting your time.

TED

Look, just come over to the studio tomorrow at 10:00 a.m. We'll see what happens. Deal?

TILLY

(Hesitant. To TED:) I'll think about it.

TED

(Shrugs.) Well, if I see you, I see you.

(TED exits spotlight).

TILLY

(To AUDIENCE:) I'm curious. Anyway, I need a job, any job. So I decide to go to the studio. I figure if Ted Andrew's not on the up and up, I'll find out soon enough. But when I arrive at the gates and give my name to the guard, he calls upstairs. Then I'm escorted to Ted Andrew's office, a large corner suite on the tenth floor. Lots of floor-to-ceiling windows. Sliding doors leading to a large balcony with fancy patio furniture, palm trees, and assorted greenery in planters.

(TED re-enters spotlight.)

TILLY

(To AUDIENCE:) When I'm seated in a black leather chair, Ted smirks. Like he's just won a trophy.

TED

(Beaming.) So you made it.

TILLY

(To TED:) As I said before, let's cut the crap and get down to business.

TED

Okay, okay.

(TED exits spotlight.)

TILLY

(To AUDIENCE:) Surprise, surprise! Ted doesn't try to seduce me. I do a screen test and get the role on *The Gathering Storm.* The studio changes my name to Leila Prince. For about two years, I play Cassandra Angelis, an "evil" woman who goes after married men with a vengeance. Cassandra's a bit unrealistic, a one-dimensional character who doesn't learn from her mistakes—she must sleep with 30 men in that one year, and yet she falls in and out of bed each time without thinking. But that's okay; I *do* have fun with the role.

(Pauses.) I like pretending to be what I am not.

(Pauses.) By Hollywood standards, my personal life's really quite dull, although I'm making lots of money, and my fan mail—most of it in the "hate" category—outnumbers the rest of the cast's combined. But I don't think too much about it; it's not ME viewers hate. In fact, I see the angry mail as a compliment. I'm the total opposite of Cassandra, who likes to flit around on the party circuit, drinking expensive cocktails, and picking up and bedding down unavailable men.

The real me just likes going home after a day's work. Put my feet up, sip Constant Comment laced with a touch of blackberry liqueur, and read a good book. Occasionally, I go to a *Storm* party or a "command performance" social event. But I'm not comfortable with that scene. So I can't understand why my name is beginning to pop up in the gossip columns, why I'm being linked with celebrity men I haven't even met.

I decide to ignore the whole thing, thinking maybe it'll all die down. People don't understand that I'm *not* Cassandra Angelis. Even Mom and Dad, who know me better than anyone else, get confused. Every so often, they'll call from Pennsylvania and ask, "What's going on out there?" I just say, "Don't worry, I haven't done anything to be ashamed of."

(Pauses.) I've become best friends with Tess, Ted's lovely wife who manages the wardrobe department. Although she runs the department like a drill sergeant, she's a devoted mother to their three boys and two girls. I especially love Emmy, Ted and Tess's three-year-old daughter. She's a pretty, self-confident child, with long auburn hair like her mother's. In between takes, I teach her how to play Candyland and Parcheesi—she's smart, too. The older girl, Ginny, looks like an older version of Emmy, but Ginny's a bit of a brat, and I avoid her. She always gets her way; when she throws a tantrum, all the makeup people stop what they're doing and cater to that child's every whim. Ginny's even made a few cameo appearances on the show as Cassandra's illegitimate child.

(Pauses.) I really hate those scenes. I don't tell Tess any of this because Ginny's obviously her favorite, and Emmy more than makes up for Ginny's naughtiness. Besides, I don't want to risk losing my friendship with Tess—or Emmy. On our days off, Tess and I—and the girls—hang out at Malibu. Swimming and

working on our tans. I don't know the boys too well; they're in school all day and rarely come to the studio.

(Pauses. Seems wistful.) I can tell Tess anything, not that there's a whole lot to tell. I don't even have a boyfriend, let alone a lover. Who has time?

(Pauses.) I begin sensing some jealousy on the *Storm* set. I'm not sure why the other cast members refuse to talk to me, and why, when I walk onto the set, people stop talking and just stare at me as if I have an extra arm or leg. Okay, so I'm not a social butterfly, and maybe some people misconstrue that as being unfriendly.

Even Tess seems a bit reticent lately—

(Pauses.) I don't know what happens with Ted but all of a sudden, he begins believing that I'm Cassandra...he starts coming onto me.

> *(TED enters spotlight with TILLY. Begins dancing around TILLY in a suggestive manner but does not touch her.)*

TILLY

(To AUDIENCE:) It seems that no matter where I turn, Ted is there, touching my hair, patting me on the rear, brushing against my chest.

(To TED.) I don't want to have an affair with you.

TED

(Freezes.) You know you want it.

TILLY

(To AUDIENCE:) See? Some men just don't get it. As he turns up the heat, rumors about my sleeping with him start flying.

TED

You might as well lie back and enjoy the inevitable.

TILLY

(To TED.) You're insufferable.

(To AUDIENCE:) By now, Tess has stopped speaking to me altogether. I wish I could talk to her, but I know that if I even insinuate her husband's a liar and womanizer, I'll lose this war—and my job. I keep thinking the whole thing will blow over, and Ted will give up and find someone else. God knows there's plenty of willing women out there. So I go out of my way to avoid Ted without alienating him and my job. But, eventually, that becomes impossible; one night, he catches up with me in the parking lot.

TED

Leila, it's time to put out or get out.

TILLY

Why now?

TED

(Shrugs.) Because I can.

(A waltz plays on the LOUDSPEAKER. TED takes TILLY into his arms, and they begin a slow dance. The spotlight follows them. Music softens.)

TILLY

(Sighs. To AUDIENCE:) Yes, now I AM sleeping with him. I have no choice if I want to keep playing Cassandra.

(Starts stroking TED's face. Obviously rationalizing.)

Sex with Ted isn't really so bad if I close my eyes and pretend that I'm Cassandra on yet another assignation. *(She kisses TED's cheek.)* He's actually a good lover, and in other circumstances—*(Pauses.)* Except for what I'm doing to Tess, the "bad girl" in me could enjoy this liaison with Ted.

(The music stops and they stop dancing. TILLY and TED kiss, and then she breaks away from TED and returns to down SC.)

(TED exits spotlight.)

TILLY

(Pulls out a compact from her pocket, opens it, and looks at herself in the mirror.)

(*To AUDIENCE:*) It's only when I look at myself do I see what I have become in the past few months: whore for hire.

(*Slams compact shut, puts it away, and brushes her arms in disgust. Then puts her hands over her eyes.*)

Now when Mom and Dad call from Pennsylvania, I dodge their questions about my personal life.

(*Looks up again and seems to pull herself together.*) For awhile, things seem to settle down a bit; I've grown used to being shunned and talked about, and I don't see Tess around anymore. She's quit her job. Life goes on, and I'm making more money than ever.

(*Pauses. Voice becomes very shaky, and she's on the verge of tears.*)

Then one day, about a year later, my entire life changes again. Just an ordinary day. I arrive for work as usual, but I'm a little early. The studio's dark, and as I feel my way through the room, my foot catches on something.

LOUDSPEAKER

(*Childlike voice.*) OW! (*Whimpering in pain.*)

(*Spotlight focuses on a red-headed doll, about the size of a three-year-old girl, all dressed in a frilly dress and ribbons in her hair, laid out flat on the floor, with blocks and other toys next to her.*)

TILLY

EMMY! Oh, sweetheart!

(Picks up the doll and holds her close. Kisses "EMMY's" cheek.)

I didn't mean to hurt you.

("EMMY" appears to be struggling.)

It's okay, It's okay. It's just Aunt Leila.

LOUDSPEAKER

("EMMY" stops struggling.)

Aunt Leila? Aunt Leila! Auntie Leila, I miss you!

TILLY

(Hugging "EMMY" even closer.) Oh, I've missed you, too. Where's your mommy?

LOUDSPEAKER

In Daddy's office.

TILLY

(To AUDIENCE:) I find that really odd; Tess hasn't been around here in months, and why would she leave Emmy here all by herself, among all these dangerous wires and plugs? It's just not

like Tess. Something must be up, and what if it has anything to do with me? I'm scared.

(Pauses.) I've got to stop being so paranoid. Whatever she's looking for, she won't find anything silly of mine, like hidden love letters.

(Pauses.) Then I get a brilliant idea, though it's too bad I don't have time to plan more carefully. Still, there's something to be said for *carpe diem.* Seizing the day. It's all so clear to me now: I'll just take Emmy away from here.

(Hugs the doll closely.) And I have enough money in the bank to pull off the caper, too. It's just a matter of getting to the money and out of the area before anyone catches on. I decide it's workable and worth giving up Cassandra for. I've always wanted my own child, and I love Emmy more than Tess ever could—besides, she can afford to give up one child out of five. Once they all get past the initial shock, who's going to notice?

(To "EMMY":) How would you like to go on a trip with Auntie Leila?

LOUDSPEAKER

Yes! Can Mommy go, too?

TILLY

(To "EMMY":) Your Mommy's going to meet us in few days.

Okay?

LOUDSPEAKER

Okay.

TILLY

(To AUDIENCE:) I hate lying to the person I love most in the world, but it's got to be done. I'll make it up to her somehow. I'm surprised how easily Emmy leaves with me. Child in tow, I get past the guard by giving some lame excuse about taking her out to breakfast. Still, I know it's only a matter of time before Tess discovers Emmy missing, speaks to the guard, and puts two and two together.

(Pauses. Becomes emotional. On the verge of crying.)

I should've known the plan was doomed. A week later, Emmy and I are picked up in Seattle, just before boarding a boat to Alaska. Two policemen arrest me and snatch Emmy away.

(Someone's hands from outside the spotlight pulls the doll away from her.)

LOUDSPEAKER

(Agonized crying.)

TILLY

(Toward the direction of the doll.) It's okay, sweetheart. We've had fun, haven't we?

LOUDSPEAKER

(Between sobs and sniffles.) Yes, Auntie. Where's Mommy?

TILLY

(To AUDIENCE:) Now I realize all too clearly just how lame and pointless this whole plot has been. I could never be Emmy's mama, no matter how long I kept and loved her.

(Pauses.) We are flown, on separate flights, back to L.A., where Emmy is reunited with the Andrews and I'm escorted to the county jail.

(Pauses.) As I await my arraignment, I think, "Wow, I was a mom for a week. What a rush!" I was a good mom, too. No one can take that away from me.

(Pauses.) Three slick lawyers on my case maneuver for temporary insanity. But I'm well-known enough that the judge and jury want to make an example of me. And Ted wields a lot of power in L.A. and lobbies hard for my incarceration. So I serve one year in prison for kidnaping, with five years probation. Had I demanded ransom, my sentence might have been mandatory life, but I wanted the child, not the money. I already had the money. When I get out of prison, I'm broke—even my house in the Hills and my furnishings have been seized and sold; my Hollywood lawyers

have attacked my savings like sharks on a feeding frenzy.

(Pauses.) So I serve my time, and leave prison with nothing, not even a prospect of a job.

(Pauses.) I'm dead meat in this town.

(Pauses. Obviously much pain in her voice.) And my parents have disowned me. I've nothing to lose now. So I go over to the studio and ask to speak with Ted, just to explain why I took Emmy. I really don't want any favors, just understanding. He agrees to see me, but I suspect he's more curious than anything.

(TED enters the spotlight and bows in a sarcastic manner.)

TED

(Stands straight up and "steeples" his hands.) So, Leila Prince, what brings you groveling back here?

TILLY

(To AUDIENCE:) I know immediately he's not about to forgive me for stealing his little girl.

(To TED.) I'm not here to ask for anything. Just to say I'm sorry. *(Tries to take TED's hand.)*

TED

(Pushes TILLY *away.)* BITCH! You can NEVER give back what you've taken from my little Emmy. We're all in therapy because of you.

TILLY

I would've NEVER harmed Emmy. You know that.

TED

(Turns away from TILLY.*)* Just get the fuck out!

TILLY

All right. *(Is really choked up here.)*

(To AUDIENCE:*)* I stand up to leave, but then a switch clicks on in my brain. There's only one way out now. I turn around, head for Ted's balcony, and slide open the glass doors. I throw myself up on the rail and straddle it.

> *(Mimes climbing up on a rail.)*

TED

(Grabs his chest and opens mouth wide—reactions are quite exaggerated.) LEILA!

TILLY

(Leans over. To AUDIENCE:*)* I ignore Ted and look down: I see toy cars parked below, toy people walking back and forth, and I

wonder how it will feel when my flesh and bones hit the macadam. Will I die on impact, or will I suffer first? With my luck, my broken flesh and bones will survive, hooked up to tubes coming in and out of every orifice, and I'll be imprisoned in a wheel chair for the rest of my life.... *(Stands up straight.)*

(TED runs toward TILLY, but she holds her hands out in front of her.)

TILLY

(To TED:) Stop right there, or I'll jump.

TED

PLEASE, Leila. Let's talk about this.

TILLY

I'm listening.

TED

(Seems very nervous and frightened.) First come inside.

TILLY

I'll stay here.

(To AUDIENCE:) You see the fear in his eyes? It really would cause an inconvenience should I throw myself off his balcony, raising even more questions and suspicions. The gossip

columnists would have a heyday with this one! What would the public say if Teddy's former soap opera star and lover flew off HIS balcony and landed on the pavement with a splat? *(Laughs.)*

(Pauses and crosses her arms. Nods her head and speaks deliberately.)

Yes. Definitely. Worth. Dying. For.

(In a controlled voice to TED:*)* I *AM* going to jump, you know.

TED
(Obviously very upset.) Oh, please, God, no. Don't do it.

TILLY
(To TED:*)* I have no dreams left, Ted. I have nothing.

TED
(Stutters. Gestures wildly.) But y-y-you have t-ta-ta-talent, you have friends.

TILLY
(Spits at TED.*)* I have nothing, you asshole. NOTHING. You've made sure of that.

(Pauses and looks out at the AUDIENCE:*)*

Looks like we've got an audience.

(Then looks straight at TED *and shouts.)* I never wanted to fuck you. You know that, don't you?

TED

Yes.

TILLY

Say it loud!

TED

YES!

TILLY

(Leans way over, her hands almost touching the floor.) Say after me, "Leila Prince never wanted to fuck Ted Andrews!"

TED

"Leila Prince never wanted to fuck Ted Andrews."

TILLY

(Still leaning over, cups her hands to her mouth) LOUDER!

TED

"LEILA PRINCE NEVER WANTED TO FUCK TED ANDREWS!"

TILLY

(Standing up straight.) Very good.

TED

(Pleading.) Now will you come inside?

TILLY

(Annoyed.) I told you I'm going to jump. It's just a matter of when. *(Leans over.)*

TED

Wait a minute!

TILLY

(Stands up.) Now, what?

TED

What will it take for you to reconsider?

TILLY

(To AUDIENCE:) I have to think hard about this one. I could ask to be taken off the black list—I could act again—maybe even ask for money, lots of it, more than enough to cover my depleted bank account.

(Pauses.) Don't think it doesn't SERIOUSLY cross my mind. But as I start to open my mouth to spell out greedy demands, a huge

bubble burps out *(Leaning toward TED.)* I can scarcely believe what tumbles out of my mouth.

(To TED:) Three things and three things only will get me off this rail:

First, I want you to write out "Leila Prince never wanted to fuck Ted Andrews in the first place" and place ads in the trade weeklies.

Second and MOST IMPORTANT, I want to see Emmy one last time, just for one hour. I'll settle for a supervised visit. And I want a clause put in there that if you don't fulfill this part of the contract within 30 days, you owe me a million bucks.

Finally, I want a loaded pistol with all registration papers in order and in my hand. IMMEDIATELY.

Then I want contracts drawn up for the first two demands and witnessed by a notary public.

TED
(Obviously pained.) First and third ones, no problem, but Tess'll never go for a visitation.

TILLY
Well, then. *(Leans over.)* I'm out of here—

TED

NO! WAIT! I'll call Tess.

(Leaves the spotlight.)

TILLY

(To AUDIENCE:) Think she'll go for it? I'm still here, aren't I?

LOUDSPEAKER

(Several VOICES IN UNISON and building up to shouts:) Jump, Jump, Jump, Jump! Jump! Jump! JUMP! JUMP! JUMP! JUMP!!!!—

(Spotlight goes down. The shouts continue, eventually fading out.)

Intermission

Take 6

(20 Minutes Later)

(Spotlight comes up and focuses down SC on TILLY.)

TILLY

(Obviously very impatient.) Wonder what's taking Ted so long?

LOUDSPEAKER

(Several VOICES IN UNISON.) JUMP!!!!

TILLY

(Leans over and cups her hand to her mouth.) FUCK OFF!

(Stands straight up. To AUDIENCE:) Impatient lot.

LOUDSPEAKER

(Ignoring TILLY. A chorus of VOICES IN UNISON.) JUMP! JUMP! JUMP! JUMP!—

TILLY

(To AUDIENCE:) Blood mongers. Too much TV. They don't realize this is REAL.

(Chant continues for a few more seconds, then TED, with papers in hand, enters spotlight. Chorus of VOICES IN UNISON stops.)

TED

(To AUDIENCE:) Whew! That woman drives a hard bargain.

(To TILLY.) All signed, sealed, and delivered. All I need is your signature.

(Holds out the gun, papers, and a pen to her.)

TILLY

(Recoils from TED.) Don't come any closer! Just put them on the floor and shove them over here.

(TED obeys.)

TILLY

That's it. Now leave, close the doors behind you, and go back to your office.

(TED exits the spotlight.)

(To AUDIENCE:) He's a slippery slime bucket, liable to pull a fast one...

("Jumps" up as if she's getting off a rail, picks up the gun, papers,

and pen and "climbs" up again. Looks over the papers.)
They seem in order.

(Shoves papers into her pocket. Poses with the gun as if she were a gunfighter. Then aims it into the air and shoots. A loud bang. She stumbles back but catches herself.)

Nice piece.

(Opens the pistol and checks the chambers.)

Six shooter.

(Closes it up again and slips it into her jacket pocket. Takes papers out and reads them again. Shuffles through them.)

One, two, three, four, five, six.... Hmmm-mmmm. Two of everything.

(Signs the papers with a flourish and takes out the pistol.)

(Shouts SL:) Okay, you can come back.

(TED enters the spotlight and walks toward TILLY.)

TILLY
(Points gun at TED.) Halt right there, honey.

TED

(Obviously afraid. Stops. Holds his hands in front of his face.) Don't shoot!

TILLY

I won't if you follow my orders exactly. Now put your hands up and turn around.

TED

(Obeys. Is shaking.) I never meant to hurt you.

TILLY

Sure. *(Mimes climbing off the rail.)*

LOUDSPEAKER

(VOICES IN UNISON grumbling with disappointment.) Aw, c'mon! JUMP! Coward! JUMP! JUMP! Chicken shit! JUMP! JUMP! JUMP! Bitch! JUMP! Slut—

TILLY

(Turns and shouts at AUDIENCE:) GHOULS!

(Walks to TED and sticks gun right in the middle of his back.)

Don't move one inch of flesh, or I'm going to blast you.

(Still pointing gun in his back, she does a body search, making sure

her hand lingers between his thighs.)
TED
OW!

TILLY
(Laughing.) Feels pretty limp now.

TED
That hurt!

TILLY
No more than I hurt.

(Jabs the gun in his back.)

Now move. One false step and you're history.

(TILLY and TED slowly exit the spotlight, which remains on.)

TILLY
(From offstage.) CLEAR THE HALLS, OR HE'S A DEAD MAN.

TED
(From offstage.) SHE MEANS IT! OH, NO, PLEASE DON'T—

(A shot reverberates from offstage. Few seconds pass. TILLY returns to the spotlight, holding the smoking pistol. She blows at the end.)

TILLY

(To AUDIENCE:) I don't kill him. I don't even shoot AT him, though, God knows, I should have. Just trying to clear a path. Too many damn people around. I *do* escape, all right, but not for long. After all, it *IS* against the law to take hostages....

(Pauses and sighs.) Once again, I plead temporary insanity. This time, I'm successful—thanks to the public defender. I'm ordered to undergo extensive psychiatric tests at the state mental hospital, but, somehow, I fall between the cracks and end up staying there five years.

(Pauses. Sniffles.) But it's all worthwhile. I get to see Emmy again. Contract's iron clad, and no one wants to pay me a million bucks, and no one wants to go to court or have this scandal blasted all over Hollywood, so Ted brings her to the hospital visiting room. I'm afraid Emmy, now almost five, won't remember me after all this time, but she does. She teaches me how to play a game called *Easy Money* and chatters about pre-school.

I'll miss her....

(Pauses. Very emotional.) When I finally get out of the hospital, I discover that I've forgotten how to survive in regular society. And I've no place to go but the streets. I'm too ashamed to go back to Pennsylvania. So for the first few days, I wander aimlessly.

(Pause.) Why didn't I jump off that balcony? I should've jumped

off the balcony, the goddamn balcony, that goddamn fuckin' balcony....

(Pauses. Less emotional, perhaps a bit fatalistic.) But, gradually, I get to know the streets, its rules for survival. It's not so bad. I begin to accept I've made some choices which have led me down this road—Now I know no other way of life. Don't WANT to know any other way—

(Pauses and shrugs.) This is life, *my* life.

> *(Puts the pistol away, straightens out her clothing, and indicates that she's about to leave the stage.)*

I suppose my jumping off the balcony was never meant to be. After all, I'm sure by now Ted has gotten his comeuppance ten times over, and I've never held any grudges against Tess.

> *(Stops. A flash of insight is evident in her face and entire body.)*

Tess? Alta Universe?

> *(Pauses to let the realization sink in. Then utter and complete shock.)*

Oh, my God!

> *(Dashes out of the spotlight.)*

THE TRASH CAN OF L.A.

(Spotlight dims and goes down.)

102

Take 7

(*Lights come up.* GINGER *enters SL, returns to down SR, and begins exercising again and, at the same time, fiddling with and texting on her mobile phone;* TONY, *with* TILLY's *contract in hand, and* OSCAR *enter SL. They seem to be looking around.*)

OSCAR

Where's Tilly?

TONY

(*Shrugs.*) Beats me.

GINGER

I saw her bawling in the ladies' room.

OSCAR

(*Shaking his head.*) I had no idea—

(TILLY *enters SL. Appears to be wiping her eyes dry.*)

OSCAR

Ah, here you are. That was an astounding performance. (*Puts his hand to his heart.*)

TILLY

(Sniffling.) Now you know the ugly, sordid truth. *(Pauses. Voice fills with emotion. Shakes her head.)* Just another Hollywood fake. A SLUT!

OSCAR

Hm-mmm. *(Scratching his chin as if in deep thought.)* How about that. *(Nods and crosses his arms.)*

(The TECHNICIAN and VIDEOGRAPHER enter SL and begin fiddling with the control panel and filming again. Pictures appear on the screens.)

TONY

That don't matter a whole lot here. *(Hands the contracts to TILLY.)* Now if you'll just sign right here—

TILLY

(Shaking her head.) I just don't think that would be a very good idea—

TONY

(Genuinely surprised.) Why not?

TILLY

Once T—, I mean, Ms. Universe, finds out who I am—

TONY

Who says she has to know? Besides, it's too late. She's already signed on the dotted line. *(Shows papers to TILLY.)* Ironclad.

OSCAR

(Unfolds his arms and puts arm around TILLY.) I think you should sign. You've got nothing to lose. *(Pauses. Touches her hair.)* Besides, Unicorn owes you.

TILLY

(Nodding.) I suppose you're right.

(Grabs the papers from TONY and looks them over.) I'll do it!

OSCAR

(Deep in thought.) In fact, we all owe you—

TONY

I need your John Henry on both copies—

OSCAR

It's Hancock.

TONY

What?

OSCAR

Hancock, not Henry.

(TONY still looks puzzled.)

OSCAR/TILLY
GOOGLE IT!

TONY
(Sighs.) Whatever.

(TILLY signs both copies and hands them to TONY.)

TONY
(Obviously pleased with himself. Beaming.) That's it.

(Hands TILLY a copy.) This's your copy.

TILLY
Thanks. *(Takes papers and stuffs them into her pocket.)*

TONY
(To TILLY.) Didja ever see that kid again?

TILLY
Excuse me?

TONY

You know, Emmy.

TILLY

(Angrily.) Does it really matter?

TONY

(Shrugs.) 'Spose not. Just curious, that's all.

OSCAR

(To TONY:) Well, put a lid on it.

TONY

(Raises his hands to his face.) No problem.

TILLY

It doesn't matter.

(Complete sadness and resignation in her voice.) Emmy died in Texas with Ted and her brothers.

(To TONY:) Didn't you say so yourself?

> *(Turns away from TONY and strolls to SR where GINGER is still exercising.)*

TONY

(Obviously confused.) I *did*? Hey, where ya goin'?

(TILLY ignores TONY. He scratches his head and starts to follow TILLY, but OSCAR pulls him back.)

OSCAR

Let her go.

TONY

But—

OSCAR

(Pats TONY on the shoulder.) I'll explain later.

TILLY

(Stops next to GINGER and studies her intently.) And Ginger....

GINGER

(Stops exercising and puts her hands on her hips. In an irritated voice.) Why are ya starin' at me like that? Don'cha have a gig at the soup kitchen, or somethin'?

TILLY

(With sadness.) I'm sorry. You reminded me of someone—

(Shakes her head as if she is coming out of a dream.) Oh, never mind.

GINGER

(Shakes her head and turns away from TILLY.) Talk about loony toons.

(Resumes exercising and texting.)

TILLY

(Returns to TONY and OSCAR. With resignation.) I guess I'm ready to get started. *(Picks up the other script from the table.)*

OSCAR

You sure?

TILLY

(Nods.) I'm sure.

OSCAR

Okay, then.

(Takes the script from her and tosses it back onto the table.)

You won't be needing that. Now, where were we? Oh, I remember. Okay, I want you to...

(Holds his chest.) Whew, I'm definitely switching to decaf.

(Gets out his handkerchief, and starts wiping his forehead.) Another antacid moment.

(Starts to leave.) I'll be back. Don't start without me.

———————

(OSCAR exits.)

TONY

Well, hurry up! We ain't got all day!

(Lights go down and screens go blank.)

———————

Take 8

(One Hour Later)

(Lights and screens come up. TONY and TILLY, both visibly frustrated, are standing down SC. TONY is running his fingers through his hair, his other hand on his hips. His tie is loosened, collar button is undone, and shirt tail is hanging out. TILLY, her hair frazzled and her posture slumped, looks as if she is on the verge of tears. GINGER, still exuding youthful energy and stamina, is still exercising and texting far SR.)

TONY

Your monologue's not working, Tilly. It don't matter what you do, it just don't feel right. It's gotta feel real.

TILLY

I'm sorry, but it *IS* real.

TONY

Mebbe so, but if it don't have that feel, *(Points his index finger at TILLY)* then, BANG! BANG! We're dead in the water.

TILLY

(Points at the VIDEOGRAPHER and TECHNICIAN:) THEY'RE

making me nervous.

TONY

(Ignores TILLY. Nervously looks around. To no one in general.) Where the hell is Oscar, anyway?

TILLY

I wish I knew.

TONY

Well, I can't wait around no more.

(Walks over to where OSCAR has dropped the script. Picks it up and flips through it.) Shit! Now he's done it!

(Notices the crumpled papers on the floor. Picks one up, straightens it out, and reads it.) That bastard!

(Picks up the rest of the crumpled pages. Returns down SC.) Sorry, babe. We're gonna hafta use the script.

TILLY

I WILL *NOT*...

TONY

(Ignores TILLY and goes far SR to GINGER. Begins to knead her shoulders and back in a provocative manner. He kisses the nape of

her neck.)

Ginger, sweetheart, go find Oscar and tell him we need him pronto.

GINGER
(She pushes TONY away. Haughtily.) You promised me a role, bub. If you double-cross me, your head'll spin....

TONY
(Distracted.) Sure, honey. I'll keep that in mind. Now go get Oscar.

GINGER
I mean it, Tony.

TONY
You get Oscar, and you'll get your role.

(GINGER takes a drink of Perrier, tosses her hair back and, walking like a runway model, exits SL.)

TILLY
She can do it, too.

TONY
Do what?

TILLY

Make your head spin. Bring you to your knees. She's—

TONY

Yeah, yeah. Don't worry about it.

TILLY

(Angrily.) I won't. It's *your* funeral!

TONY

(Ignores her anger. Looks TILLY up and down.) Hm-mmmm. *(Shakes his head.)* Maybe it's the look. *(Points at the pegboard where the old clothes are hanging.)* Get those clothes on.

TILLY

I will *NOT!*

TONY

That's okay. We'll worry about your wardrobe later.

TILLY

(Moves toward the chair where her cape is draped.) I'll just be on my way.

TONY

(Pulls TILLY back.) No, WAIT! *(Hangs tightly onto TILLY. Shouts.)* OSCAR!!!! Where the hell *IS* he, anyway?

(To the AUDIENCE:) Damn! What'll I do now?

TILLY

(Struggles to break free.) Let me go!

TONY

You old hag! You signed a contract!

TILLY

I don't care!

> *(While TONY and TILLY continue their struggle, a dejected-looking GINGER, clutching her mobile phone, enters SL and moves toward the struggling pair. Pauses and watches for a few seconds.)*

GINGER

(Shouts.) He's dead!

> *(TONY and TILLY freeze. Disbelief and horror are evident in their faces.)*

TILLY/TONY

(Still frozen in place.) WHAT?

GINGER

I said, Mr. Fishbein's dead.

(TONY *releases* TILLY *and hangs his head, his arms drooping by his side.*)

TILLY

(Places her hand over her heart.) I don't believe it!

GINGER

(Sighs.) It's true. The janitor just found him a few minutes ago. All sprawled out in a pool of coffee, cold as a fish.

TONY

Where, for God's sake?

GINGER

Vending room, near the coffee machine. *(To* TILLY.*)* He's still there if you want to see for yourself. I already called 9-11, but it's obviously too late.

(TILLY *begins sobbing and buries her face in her hands. She exits SL.)*

GINGER

(Sighs.) Look, I've got to go tell Mother before the paramedics leave. *(Exits SL.)*

TONY

(Head still down, he paces around the stage, playing with his tie.)

Goddamn! What next?

(Then lifts his head as if he has come to a sudden flash of insight.) Alta Universe? Ginger's mother?

(Pauses as if he is trying to absorb this new information.)

Oh, no! *(Slaps his forehead and runs off stage, screaming.)*

(The lights go down and screens go off.)

Take 9

(Spotlight comes up down SC. Draped in a bright glittery cape with matching gown, THE DIVINE MS. ALTA UNIVERSE stands frozen in a tableau fashion. She should come across as a new-age Goddess, a regal, inaccessible woman, perhaps even on a pedestal. A cheerful ghostly OSCAR enters and roams the stage. The spotlight widens, and the lights slowly come up. The VIDEOGRAPHER and TECHNICIAN enter, and the screens come to life, but only ALTA's picture appears on screen.)

OSCAR
(Walks around in his usual energetic manner, except he does not grab at his chest. To the AUDIENCE:)

Don't know what was in that brew, but I feel younger than ever.

(Dances a little jig.)

Haven't been able to do that in years. I'm going to buy that coffee machine and move to South America with Tilly. Mrs. Fishbein will be happy to be rid of me. Life'll be grand.

(Pauses. Confidentially to the AUDIENCE:) First, I've got some loose ends to tie up, some amends to make, some lobbying to do.

(To ALTA:) Look, Ms. Universe, about that conversion scene? I know it's a very religious and sentimental piece close to your heart, and I had no business ripping up the script, but it's not Tilly at all. All I'm asking is that you give her a fair chance to strut her real stuff.

(Pauses.) About that old baggage? She never meant to hurt you. Why, she didn't even WANT to sleep with your husband.

   (Waits for response but gets none.)

(Shrugs.) Just ask her. As for Emmy...well, our Tilly didn't hurt the child, did she?

   (Pauses for an answer, but gets no response.)

I'll do anything you want.

   (Pauses and swallows hard.)

Anything.

(Confidentially to the AUDIENCE:) It's a good thing she wouldn't like—what was it Tilly called me?—an aging Lothario? Still, even *I* have a few scruples left, but I wouldn't want *her (Nods toward ALTA.)* to suspect my weaknesses.

   (To ALTA:)

You should've seen her today, the way she expressed herself.

(Seems to be speaking more to himself now. Moves around and gestures a lot.)

Her struggle with death, how she conquered it. Her fear of it, I mean. After all, we never conquer death itself, do we? Though we deny it to the end. Still, the fight's everything because what else is there?

(Pauses.) She could've ended all her misery that day on the balcony. Fallen to the ground like a wounded bird, releasing a broken spirit....But something, a thin filament—dare I say hope?—stopped her from jumping that day.

(Shivers.) It's so cold in here. *(Pauses. Practically in ALTA's face.)* So how about it?

(ALTA ignores him.)

Well, can't blame you for hating me. I'm a real jackass sometimes.

(Pauses. Shrugs and laughs.) So I like women, especially young and nubile ones. An aging Lothario.

(Pauses.) But not to worry, I don't have evil designs on your Ginger—

(Seems puzzled that he has gotten no response from ALTA by now.)

Though I'm not so sure about Tony Thornton—

(Still no response.)

I'd watch him if I were you. He's definitely headed for the sheets with Ginger.

(Still nothing. Is now alarmed).

(Shouts.) IN FACT, HE'S SCREWING YOUR DAUGHTER EVERY CHANCE HE GETS! *(Pauses.)*

(No reaction at all from ALTA.)

(Obviously alarmed.) Oh, my God. You really can't hear me at all!

(Waves his hand directly in front of her face. ALTA blinks as if she feels a draft. OSCAR backs away.)

What's going on?

(He looks down at his hands.) What's this? I can see through them. I'm disappearing....

(OSCAR begins fading out.)

Oh, no, it just can't be, please, not yet—

(Shouts.) TILLY!

(Lights go down and screens fade to black.)

Take 10

(One Week Later)

(The lights come up. The stage is rearranged—the pegboard, jewelry, and coffeepot are gone—and everything is straightened up. The table, now empty—except for two brand new scripts—still has the Langston Hughes poster taped to it.)

(A brand new silver galvanized garbage can dominates down SC. It is important that the garbage can be new, perhaps with its label still glued to it.)

(The two folding chairs and the director's chair are scattered about. On one of the folding chairs is draped TILLY's fur cape.)

(TONY, who is wearing a different suit, shirt, and tie, and GINGER, who is dressed in the old clothes—dress, sweater, straw hat, and socks—that had been hanging on the pegboard and the old galoshes, enter and head down SC. She carries the bag with appliquéd daisies and a bottle of Ripple, or any cheap wine, under her arm. Her hair is pulled back into a severe bun. The TECHNICIAN and VIDEOGRAPHER follow and begin setting up equipment. Starts rolling the camera just as soon as the equipment is set up.)

GINGER

I still can't believe how many people were at the funeral. Must've been thousands. You see my picture on *E.T.*? *(Sets the bag and wine bottle next to the garbage can.)*

TONY

(Sighs.) Yeah, for the umpteenth time, I saw it.

GINGER

Still can't believe he was famous and I didn't even know it.

TONY

Well, he was hot before your time.

GINGER

Oh, Tony, I'm so hot right now. Kiss me again.

(Sighing, TONY takes GINGER into his arms and kisses her, though his ardor does not seem to match what it had been the previous week.)

GINGER

(Pulling away.) You can do better than that.

TONY

(Annoyed.) It's just we have so much work to do and so little time—

GINGER

Don't worry, Mother'll understand.

TONY

(Sarcastically.) Sure she will.

TILLY

(TILLY, dressed entirely in black—including a black hat with veil—enters. As she tiptoes toward the chair with the cape, she trips over TONY's chair and falls onto the floor. TONY and GINGER jump and turn around. TONY rushes over to TILLY and begins helping her up.)

(Embarrassed as she allows TONY to help her.)

Thanks. *(Brushes off her clothing and throws back the veil.)*

TONY

(Puts his arm around her shoulder.) You okay?

TILLY

(Sheepishly.) Yeah.

TONY

Well, good. Just the same, stop by the infirmary—

TILLY

Oh, I'm fine.

TONY

(To the AUDIENCE:) Yeah, how much you wanna bet a lawyer'll come around and slap the studio with a big accident/injury suit?

(Annoyed, to TILLY:)

Whaddya doin' here, anyway? Didn't Ms. Universe shell out enough to buy back your contract?

TILLY

(Apologetically.) She was very generous. I'm just here to pick up the cape I left here last week, you know, in all the confusion.

TONY

(Embarrassed.) Oh. I see.

(Turns away from TILLY, grabs the scripts from the table, and goes back to GINGER. The two stand on either side of the garbage can.)

TILLY

I'll be on my way now. *(But she remains in place.)*

TONY

(Ignoring TILLY. To GINGER.) Now, sweetheart, let's do the conversion scene.

GINGER

But—

TONY

(Sarcastically.) Mother's orders.

(The ghostly OSCAR enters and takes his place next to TILLY. Even as a ghost, he can't stand still.)

OSCAR

(To TILLY.) You oughta stick around for a few laughs.

TILLY

(Doesn't see or hear OSCAR. Shivers.) There's a draft in here.

(TILLY picks her cape up and puts it around her shoulders. Starts to leave.)

OSCAR

WAIT! *(Tries to grab TILLY's arm, but all he gets is air).*

(To the AUDIENCE:) I'll never get used to this afterlife crap. It was bad enough when no one listened to me. Now, no one *hears* or *sees* me anymore. *(Shrugs.)* But what choice do I have?

TILLY

(Stops and turns around. Walks down SL. TONY and GINGER do not

even notice her.)

(To the AUDIENCE:*)* Maybe I'll just stick around for a few laughs. *(Partially hides behind the screen SL.)*

OSCAR

(Jumps up and down. Then makes a fist and does a chop.) YES!

> *(Skipping across stage, he joins* TONY *and* GINGER. *He stands behind the garbage can, between the other two characters. During the following scene, he will react to the ongoing action by miming body language in an exaggerated manner, for example, folding his arms, hitting his forehead, laughing—silently—jumping up and down, frowning, etc.)*

TONY

(Hands GINGER *one of the scripts. Flips through the other copy.)* Let's start on page 45. *(Looks around.)* Where's that bottle?

GINGER

(Picks up the Ripple bottle and holds it up.) Right here. *(Assumes a sexy pose.)*

TONY

(Ignores GINGER'S *behavior.)* Okay. Middle of the page. *(Points out the place to* GINGER.*)*

GINGER

Oooh, this is so much fun.

TONY

(Irritated.) Now, let's get serious.

GINGER

(Blows him a kiss.) Oh, yes. Let's!

TONY

(Ignoring her actions.) In this scene, Tilly the bag lady, is drunk as hell. She's standing over the trash can—

GINGER

Oh, this is so-oo-oooo stupid. *(But she poses over the garbage can, swaying like a drunkard. Shoves the bottle toward TONY.)* Do's youse wanna wittle dwinkie?

TONY

Good, good. Now you're getting into character. Okay. Tilly's at a crisis in her life. She's gotta decide what she's gonna do. Will she suck down that cheap bottle of wine or, like, find Jesus Christ?

GINGER

(Giggling.) This is rich.

TONY

(Exasperated.) Your mother's idea.

GINGER

(Sighs and rolls her eyes back.) Figures. *(Becomes serious.)* So let's get on with it.

TONY

Good. Now, I'll read the part of Tilly's sponsor. *(Looks at the VIDEOGRAPHER.)* Hey, [ACTOR's name]! Focus on Ginger, not me! *(The screens now show only GINGER.)* Okay, here goes.

> *(Puts his hand on his heart. Is obviously overacting. Booms in a dramatic, deep voice.)*

"Tilly, Tilly. It's up to you. Toss that evil brew into the garbage."

GINGER

> *(Holds the bottle over the garbage can. Her hand starts to shake. She licks her lips. The entire scene is played out in a campy sort of way.)*

"I-I-I d-d-don'-don't know. I want it so badly."

TONY

"Try, Tilly."

> *(He clasps her raised hand and the two remained locked like this for*

several seconds.)

OSCAR/TILLY

Appalling!

TONY

(Still clasping GINGER's hand.) "You have no choice, Tilly. If you don't rid yourself of the devil's grip, you will surely die. Let go, and accept Jesus Christ as your personal savior, and you will be saved! Your life will fall into the middle way. The GOOD and Godly way."

GINGER

(Stops shaking and relaxes a bit. Looks up to the heavens.) "Jesus?" *(Places her hand on her heart, but still hangs onto the bottle.)*

TONY

"You *must* let go or you will just be another lost soul. Like Annie. You remember Annie?"

GINGER

(Nods. Starts weeping.) "Yes! I remember."

TONY

"Tell me. What happened to Annie?"

GINGER

(Still weeping.) "She died like a stray dog in the gutter."

(Draws the bottle back and seems to look at it in a new light. Shows it to the AUDIENCE.)

"She was found naked with one of these stuck in her mouth."

TONY

(Looks at the AUDIENCE:) "What a horrible death! *(Back to Ginger:)* Now you know what you must do. Let go of that bottle now, Tilly."

GINGER

(Slowly raises the bottle into the air, but continues to clasp it. Begins shaking again.)

"I never wanted to become this way, a drunk and a slut—a receptacle for strange, foul men. I only wanted to be a normal woman.

(Pauses.) Marry. Give birth to perfect babies, keep a beautiful home, maybe have a rewarding career. But, but, alas! Things just did not work out. And it's all my fault."

TONY

(Dramatically.) "And what will you be doing about it?"

OSCAR/TILLY

(TILLY runs out from behind the screen, and OSCAR meets her halfway. OSCAR "holds" TILLY's hand, and they stand SL of TONY and GINGER. In a mimicky, sarcastic chorus:)

And what will you be doing about it?

And what will you be doing about it?

And what will you be doing about it?

Tell me, Tilly, darling, what will you be doing about it?

Will you be throwing away that evil booze and accepting Jesus Christ as your personal savior?

Or will you be joining poor old Annie, dead in the gutter, her soul burning eternally in hell?

Tell me, soon, Tilly love, I can wait no longer,

This story's far too long as it is,

So what will you be doing about it?

(TONY and GINGER are stunned. Both just stand there, frozen, their mouths hanging wide open, as TILLY goes over to GINGER.

(OSCAR watches with amusement.)

TILLY

Well, *I* know what *I'll* be doing about it!

(Grabs the bottle from GINGER's raised hand and guzzles down the entire bottle. Tosses the empty into the garbage can.)

Ahhhh! *That's* what *I* did about it.

(Sings.) Hi, Ho, Hi, Ho. Off to hell we go, hi, ho, hi, ho—

(Repeats two or three times. OSCAR joins in the second chorus. In the middle of the last chorus, both begin to leave the stage. TILLY pauses at the table and then carefully removes the Langston Hughes poster from the table. Finishes up last chorus with OSCAR. Moves down SL. Then reads to the AUDIENCE:)

"Hold fast to dreams, for if dreams die, life is a broken winged bird that cannot fly." Langston Hughes. I guess that about sums it up.

(Rolls up the poster, and tucks it under her arm. Looks around.) It really *is* drafty in here.

(Looks directly at OSCAR. Seems momentarily surprised— she obviously sees him now—but quickly recovers her composure. Places her fist on her chest and smiles. Walks over to OSCAR. He kisses

her forehead, and she takes his hand and kisses it.)

C'mon, darling, let's blow this joint.

(OSCAR and TILLY exit SL, arm in arm. TONY and GINGER, rubbing their eyes, look as if they have just awakened from a bad dream.)

GINGER
(Pointing SC.) Look, Tony. That old bag stole that bird poster!

TONY
Well, I'll be damned!

(House lights go dark.)

The Wrap

(The stage remains dark, for all action takes place on the screens. The screens come on, and fade in. The program opens with STREET SHOCK! scrolling across the screens, and bold music, perhaps a current pop song. Street scenes appear on screen, changing about every five seconds. Intermittent "Take 1" scenes of TILLY, whose face is "scrambled," flash onto the screen in between the street scenes. OSCAR's street part has been edited out. While these scenes are being shown, the credits are rolling by, each name scrolling across the screen for a few seconds before fading into the next name:)

Starring...

Ginger Universe: Anonymous Homeless Woman

Anthony Thornton: Narrator

Oscar Fishbein: Interviewer

[Male Actor's real name]: as himself

Anthony Thornton: Director

Videographer: [real name]

Technician: [real name]

Oscar Fishbein: Screenwriter

(After the credits are shown, the program, which consists of some obviously edited clips of TONY*'s stilted interview with* TILLY *just as they took place in the studio and other added material, begins.* TILLY*'s face, however, is scrambled, just like in some popular reality-based TV shows.)*

TONY

Anthony Thornton reporting for Unicorn Studios. I have here with me today Ms. BLEEP!—who wishes to remain anonymous— of, ha, ha, no fixed address, is that right?

TILLY

(Voice electronically altered.) Yes.

TONY

Could you tell our viewing audience why that is, Ms. BLEEP!?

TILLY

You may call me BLEEP!, Tony. It's okay. To answer your question, I'm homeless. I live on the streets of L.A. I guess you could call me a bag lady because all I own can be found in this satchel—*(Holds it up.)*

TONY

Truly an American tragedy!

TILLY

(Turns around. Is visibly upset. Crosses her arms and faces TONY.)
DAMN RIGHT IT IS!

(Fade out. Fade in. TONY is outside standing on a city sidewalk, holding a microphone.)

TONY

How could this horrible tragedy happen in our very own United States of America? Just before he passed on, *(voice lowers in "respect")* God rest his soul, *(raises voice again)* Oscar Fishbein got an exclusive interview with BLEEP! in which she tells all about her life of misery and the job from hell! The job that was supposed to put her on her feet financially, but, instead, sent her packing to the streets of L.A.! This lurid tale of degradation in the work place will surely break your heart. *(Confidentially.)* To protect all parties involved, the name of the club has been deleted. We pick up the interview when BLEEP! tells Mr. Fishbein the day her spiral to the gutter began.

(Fade out. Fade in.)

TILLY

(Again, face scrambled and voice electronically altered.) I answered an ad in the *L.A. Free Press (Assumes dramatic pose.)*: "Wanted: BLEEEEEP! for the BLEEP! Club. Got the job immediately.

OSCAR

How about that.

TILLY

Within a week, I got fired.

OSCAR

(Pats TILLY's hand.) Well, what happened?

TILLY

An old man—at least 60—grabs my *(points to her chest)* and starts licking. I'm, like, in shock and just stand there taking it. When I finally come to my senses and push him away, he slaps me and says, "A whore." *(Starts to sob.)*

OSCAR

(Puts his arms around TILLY and comforts her.) Hey, hey. It's okay.

TILLY

He thought I was hooking on the side. Can you imagine? The worst part, my boss wouldn't listen. So, okay, fire me. *(Pauses.)*

You know, I never worked after that. Went right from the lounge to the street.

OSCAR

It wasn't your fault. And BLEEP!?

TILLY

Hmmm?

OSCAR

You WILL be heard loud and clear!

(Fade out. Fade in. Back on the street with TONY *and the microphone.)*

TONY

Her voice deserves to be heard, and you're hearing it exclusively here on *Street Shock*. After that debacle in the club, our unsung heroine went from respectable working girl to the lowest scum of the gutter. Prostitution, drugs, alcohol—you name it, she did it. And then something very interesting happened. In her interview with Mr. Fishbein, our heroine revealed an important turning point in her life, an epiphany. Because of its sensitive nature, we have reconstructed the scene using actors. To protect her identity, our heroine's name has been changed to "Leila."

(Fade out. Fade in.)

*(*GINGER, *who is wearing the same bag lady clothes as she had on in the studio, and a* MALE ACTOR, *who is dressed in a suit and tie, are outside on a city street. A beat up rusty can is between them.* GINGER *holds the bottle over the garbage can. Unlike before, this part is played "straight," although the hokey dialogue itself is*

probably beyond "saving.")

MALE ACTOR
"Leila, Leila. It's up to you. Toss that evil brew into the garbage."

GINGER
(Holds the bottle over the garbage can. Her hand starts to shake. She licks her lips.) "I-I-I d-d-don'-don't know. I want it so badly."

MALE ACTOR
"Try, Leila."

(He clasps her raised hand and the two remained locked like this for several seconds.)

(Still clasping GINGER's hand.) "You have no choice, Leila. If you don't rid yourself of the devil's grip, you will surely die. Let go, and accept Jesus Christ as your personal savior, and you will be saved! Your life will fall into the middle way. The GOOD and Godly way."

GINGER
(Stops shaking and relaxes a bit. Looks up to the heavens.) "Jesus?" *(Places her hand on her heart, but still hangs onto the bottle.)*

MALE ACTOR
"You *must* let go or you will just be another lost soul. Like Annie.

You remember Annie?"

GINGER
(Nods. Starts weeping.) "Yes! I remember."

MALE ACTOR
"Tell me. What happened to Annie?"

GINGER
(Still weeping.) "She died like a stray dog in the gutter."

(Draws the bottle back and seems to look at it in a new light. Shows it to the camera.)

"She was found naked with one of these stuck in her mouth."

MALE ACTOR
(Looks at the camera.) "What a horrible death! Now you know what you must do. Let go of that bottle now, Leila."

GINGER
(Slowly raises the bottle into the air, but continues to clasp it. Begins shaking again.)

"I never wanted to become this way, a drunk and a slut—a receptacle for strange, foul men. I only wanted to be a normal woman."

(Pauses.) Marry. Give birth to perfect babies, keep a beautiful home, maybe have a rewarding career. But, but, alas! Things just did not work out. And it's all my fault."

MALE ACTOR
(Dramatically.) "And what will you be doing about it?"

(Loud sound. Lightning. Thunder. Crackling—like radio static. A bright strobe light flashes on stage and a smoke machine pumps out swirling smoke. Smoke machine is shut off.)

(Fireworks displays are shown on the screens. Fade out.)

(On screen, fade into OSCAR's smiling face. The camera zeros in on him until just his mouth is on screen. On stage, more loud sound. Lightning. Thunder. Crackling Strobe lights.)

OSCAR'S MOUTH
(Deep, echoing God-like voice:) Move along, folks. Nothing here for you.

(Fade out. Fade in to credits and blaring pop music. The credits roll by quickly. Then a VOICE OVER as the unicorn symbol appears on screen:)

VOICE OVER
Street Shock is filmed at Unicorn Studios in Los Angeles,

California, and on location.

(Music stops abruptly. Fade out to black screen. Total silence. Then the following message appears on screen:)

VIDEO SCREEN
"In memory of Oscar Fishbein"

(The message remains there for several seconds before going dark.)

CURTAIN

(After curtain, the house lights come up and screens come on, and as the ACTORS take their bows, credits—just as they appear in the playbill—roll by, accompanied by the same music that played during the "Prequel")

Playwright's
Notes on Characters

Tilly Zeace
(Homeless Woman)

TILLY ZEACE is in her early to mid 40's, but she looks slightly older than she is. In "Take 1," she looks very scruffy and grungy: her long graying hair hangs free, and she's dressed in torn blue jeans and shabby white gauze blouse that has obviously seen better days. She is barefoot.

TILLY's stage appearance changes dramatically: although she wears expensive clothing for the rest of the play, there is something shabby and "exaggerated" about her appearance, yet there is an undefinable elegance in the way she carries herself. Her clothing is definitely out of style, for she wears a classic dark blue suit, cream blouse, off-white gloves, nylons, black pumps, and a fur cape. She wears her hair in a tight bun on top of her head. She wears some jewelry, but not very much: what she does wear looks as if it made of real gold, silver, and gems. By the same token, she wears rubber bands around her wrists (and pulls at them all the time). Also, her suit is spotted with lint, her blouse slightly soiled, her cape missing patches of fur, and her pumps slightly scuffed. Her nylons have some runs. She carries a brown scuffed-up satchel, crammed full of junk, with the initials "T.O.Z." Some of her papers poke through the top and sides.

TILLY has a mobile phone, but it makes an appearance only during "Take 1"; it rings on stage—she doesn't answer it—but once she shuts it down, it remains out of sight for the rest of the play.

Oscar Fishbein
(Screenwriter)

OSCAR FISHBEIN, somewhere in his 60's, is in constant motion; he can't seem to sit still for one moment, and he constantly drinks coffee. He's always touching the women around him—patting their hair, touching their shoulders, and brushing slightly against them—but never in an obvious way so that a woman could ever really challenge his actions.

OSCAR is rumpled-looking. He is very thin and wears baggy clothes: a plaid shirt—the sleeves rolled up to his elbows—with striped tie and gray jeans that are obviously too big. He wears black army boots, which are obviously from the Goodwill. His abundant salt and pepper curly hair is uncombed, slightly too long, and perhaps a bit unwashed. He could probably pass as one of TILLY's street friends.

He owns no technology—no use for it.

Tony Thornton
(Producer/Director of Street Shock)

TONY THORNTON is in his early 30's. He comes across as a bit too enthusiastic, definitely phony and slick. He is obviously a clever man, but does not come across as being a well-educated person. There is a crispness about him that would remind one of a used car salesman, but his suit is tailored and well-cut in the style of the day. He is not flashy, but rather conservative looking: well-scrubbed and freshly shaved, sporting a fashionable hair cut. It is important that his tie look "tight" around his neck, and his lips should seem thin and rigid.

He wears an older model of mobile phone on his belt, often "answering" or texting when he is on stage but not speaking and not at the center of a scene. For some scenes, as he enters the stage, he can be seen holding the phone at his ear, perhaps shouting some banality or non sequitur at the "listener" on the other end, or texting.

This addition would be at the discretion of the director; however, this play has little to do with mobile phones—only to the extent that technology in general has changed the popular culture.

Videographer
(Actor's real name)

THE VIDEOGRAPHER, any age and either gender, has no lines—
he or she simply comes on stage, sets up equipment, "mimes"
directions, and walks around with a camera (technology of the
day), recording all the action going on. Except for when he/she
first arrives on stage, rarely do the other characters pay any
attention to this person, other than to bark occasional orders. The
audience should be aware that this character is present and
recording many of the events, but the VIDEOGRAPHER should
not call undue attention to him/herself. This actor should have
some experience handling technology and should know stage
direction well. Quite possibly, the VIDEOGRAPHER could be the
director or tech person. After first entrance, the VIDEOGRAPHER
remains on stage most of the time, filming everything (except
during "Take 5" and "Take 6," and "The Wrap").

Technician
(Actor's real name)

The TECHNICIAN, any gender and any age, does actual on-stage tech work, making sure that all the equipment (stage cameras and panels) is working properly. Like the VIDEOGRAPHER, he/she works in both the real and scripted worlds in that once he arrives, he remains on stage as both techie and actor (except during "Take 5" and "Take 6," and "The Wrap")

Ginger
(Young actress)

GINGER is in her early 20's and exudes the essence of bimbo very well, coming across as shallow and rather self-absorbed. She is statuesque, lively, and beautiful, having wavy auburn hair to her waist. She wears a shiny green spandex workout suit with matching sweatband on her forehead and the latest running shoes. She wears the latest version of a mobile phone, either on a sash or hooked to her spandex. She drinks Perrier from the bottle; in short, GINGER looks as though she has just walked off the *Jersey Shore* set (or any pop culture show of the day featuring young, nubile women, albeit brainless).

Throughout her background scenes. she should be seen yakking on her phone via a blue tooth or latest technology (or texting), but none of her conversation should be heard by the AUDIENCE.

Ted Andrews
(Producer/Director of *The Gathering Storm*)

TED ANDREWS is about 30 years old. He's tall and muscular, with neatly cut hair and a Hollywood bronze complexion—in short, a very appealing man. He's soft spoken, polite, and clean-cut; he would really stand out in the days of long hair, peace buttons, and torn bell bottoms. Although not mandatory, the same actor may be used for the "MALE ACTOR" in the closing "Wrap" video, but he should be made to look different from Ted.

He is from the past, so he bears no technology on his person.

The Divine Ms. Alta Universe
(Owner, Unicorn Studios)

THE DIVINE MS. ALTA UNIVERSE makes a cameo appearance. Tall and statuesque—perhaps in her fifties—she is a commanding figure. She wears a flowing cape and gown with glittery gold and silver stars—perhaps a new-age version of the fairy godmother. Around her neck is a necklace made of chalcedonies—rose, white, and blue quartz crystals. Her auburn hair is piled elegantly on her head, and a tiara with gemstones is an integral part of her hairstyle.

Male Actor

(Actor in episode of *Street Shock*)

The MALE ACTOR, who is in his 30's and acts as Ginger's sponsor, is billed by the actor's real name. This part may be played TED's actor but this is not mandatory.

In any case, he should look very different from TED and TONY.

Suggested Set Design
The Trash Can of L.A.

The set is a TV studio in disarray. There should be a large sign in plain view that says, "Unicorn Studios," with a logo suggesting a unicorn. There are two large flat-screen TVs on stage (far SL and far SR) and several located at various points in the theatre for optimal view by the audience. For a studio or small theatre production, fewer screens would be sufficient. A computer and a control panel on stage acts as a central hub for the TVs and other on-stage cameras and are operated by a TECHNICIAN, who works directly on stage.

A small wire trash can, one designed for scrap paper and other office-type trash, should be one of the props that remains on stage during the entire play.

As play goers take their seats, city scenes from *Street Shock* (a Unicorn production) should be shown, including the credits, action, music, dialogue, etc. The director and players should create his/her own videos, showing "vignettes" from *Street Shock*, perhaps with another set of actors, or simply people from behind the scenes or from the community, in close-up shots, ad-libbing. These scenes should come across as realistic. After "Take 1" is completed, the screens should go blank, until the VIDEO-

GRAPHER arrives and begins recording scenes from the stage action. At that point, random shots should appear on the screen: close-ups and long shots of TILLY, TONY, OSCAR, and GINGER. However, it is important that these screens be out of the way of the actors, perhaps on the extreme right and left; while the TV screens are important, they should not be the main focus of the action.

At stage center is a long table filled with garish costume jewelry; buried underneath the pile are two ragged scripts. A drip coffee maker, filled with some evil-looking brew, a sloppy sugar bowl, a jar of crusted creamer, a ceramic mug—the kind that can be found in greasy spoon diners—and a stack of foam cups sit off to the side (SL). Taped to the table is a poster with birds in flight, which says, "Hold fast to dreams, for if dreams die, life is a broken winged bird that cannot fly.—Langston Hughes." On SR of the card table is a director's chair, and on SL of the table are two folding chairs. Just beyond the card table (SL) is a free-standing pegboard, with parts of a costume hung on hooks: an old worn dress, now faded but having once been a flashy, garish garment; a straw hat decorated with old campaign and peace buttons; a moth-eaten sweater; and several pairs of socks with holes. On the floor (toward SL) is a plastic shopping bag with appliquéd daisies. Also toward SL is an old pair of galoshes, the plastic opaque kind with loops and buttons. "No Smoking" signs are strategically placed all over the area. Further SL and close to the AUDIENCE is another folding chair. Finally, for effect, a bare light bulb may be dangled over the card table, casting a strange hue over the players.

Characters enter and exit the stage SL—although the DIRECTOR is free to tweak this.

*

NOTE: The DIRECTOR does have some latitude as to stage set and blocking, as long as changes do not materially change the meaning and purpose of this play.

Minor changes in stage directions are allowable, assuming that such changes would not materially change the overall meaning.

References to popular culture of the day should be tweaked.

For example, in "Take 2," the reference to Kim Kardashian should be replaced by a current trending celebrity. Popular culture references should be revised to reflect the current landscape.

In other words, this play is forever set in the present; therefore, references to popular culture and social media should be updated to reflect current fads.

Drama Notes

The Trash Can of L.A.

In *The Trash Can of L.A.*, the three main characters—TILLY, OSCAR, and TONY—grapple with the issue of "reality" versus "fiction" as it pertains to a reality-based television series. For TONY, reality is best achieved when it is manipulated into a script and strictly controlled, *but* it must have the *appearance* of being real, for example, hand-held camera shots and angles, method acting, etc. On the other hand, TILLY believes that reality—and truth—can best be achieved by simply filming the action as it happens and allowing the unedited result speak for itself. OSCAR falls somewhere in the middle of these two views. Video plays a very strong role in this play, both in practical and symbolic terms. For example, the lack of recording during TILLY's monologue is especially important in that what is "real" is lost and is never captured again. Also, a VIDEOGRAPHER is present for most of the scenes and freely shoots scenes—perhaps the most real parts of the play to be captured on film—which are then are shown on screens throughout the play. Since there are only general guidelines for this role, the VIDEOGRAPHER wields much power in what he/she decides what to shoot. Thus, each performance of the play would leave its own mark, its individual flavor, its utter reality. Thematically, this distinction is important, for the VIDEO-GRAPHER counterpoints the ongoing conflict between TILLY and TONY, for the use of video can be both real and unreal.

Also, the specific scenes, dialogue, and music—which are shown on the screens before and after curtain—are strictly up to the director and VIDEOGRAPHER. Thus, "theatre people" have an opportunity to "experiment" with another genre. Certainly, the line between "stage acting" and "TV acting" has been purposely blurred, since both occur in this play. But, alas, in the end, TV wins out—or does it?

In part, the playwright wrote this play in response to the glut of "reality-based" shows that have appeared on television in the past 30 years and particularly throughout the 21st Century. One suspects that many of the so-called "scenes-as-they-unfold" TV shows have been heavily edited, and, in some cases, even fully scripted. One can never really know what goes on behind the scenes—unless one is there.

Thus, *The Trash Can of L.A.* simply reflects one playwright's best guess—and suspicion.

Summary

The Trash Can of L.A.

In this tragicomedy, a homeless woman and an ambitious producer of a reality-based TV show clash when their interpretations of reality differ. The woman, hired to portray her own life, translates reality literally, while the producer insists on a script—no matter the actual truth. Despite his own conflicts, a washed-up screenwriter attempts to mediate between the feuding woman and producer.

About the Playwright

JENNIFER SEMPLE SIEGEL is author of *Are You EVER Going to be Thin?* (and other stories), *Memoir Madness: Driven to Involuntary Commitment*, and *The Trash Can of L.A.* (A Reality Play).

She has taught Creative Writing and Literature at York College of Pennsylvania and Ss. Cyril and Methodius University of Skopje (Skopje, Macedonia).

Her fiction and non-fiction, including scholarly articles, have been published in various national and regional journals, magazines, and anthologies. From 1993-1996, she edited *Onion River Review*, a literary journal.

She earned her M.F.A. in fiction from Goddard College (Plainfield, Vermont).

In 2009, Semple Siegel served as a Fulbright Scholar in Skopje, Macedonia.

In addition to her teaching and own writing, her Fulbright project included helping to develop a new American Studies program at Ss. Cyril and Methodius University.

She currently lives in Pennsylvania with her husband Jerry.

For more information, go to her Amazon Author Central page:

www.Jennifer.BanMyBook.com

For More Information: Jennifer@BanMyBook.com

www.ingramcontent.com/pod-product-compliance
Lightning Source LLC
Chambersburg PA
CBHW071533040426
42452CB00008B/1000